EVERYTHING
YOU NEED
YOU HAVE

EVERYTHING YOU NEED YOU HAVE

HOW TO BE AT HOME IN YOUR SELF

GERAD KITE

FOREWORD BY ANDY PUDDICOMBE, HEADSPACE

HARMONY
BOOKS • NEW YORK

To Anne
With all my love

CONTENTS

THE WORLD OF MIND

THE WORLD OF BODY

THE WORLD OF HOME

No matter who we are, where we live, what name we go by; no matter the language we speak, the culture we embrace, or the beliefs we cherish; no matter our education, our work, our views or philosophy; the ultimate journey is one of awareness and compassion; our home, right here, in this moment, one and the same place all.

"Everything You Need You Have" is a timeless message. But it is not enough to simply read the words in this book. We need to explore the essence of these words, to reflect upon them and apply this understanding to our life. In short, we must know these words not as an idea, but as an experience. Only then will we understand their true value.

Like the light from the sun, awareness illuminates our life, allowing us to see clearly, with a sense of confidence, ease and perspective; and like the warmth from the sun, compassion enriches our life, allowing us to embrace this shared human condition, with empathy, kindness and love. Ultimately, this sunlight and warmth are not separate, they are one and the same thing.

When we meet each new moment with awareness, we are free; free from the shackles of the past, free from the fears of the future; free from our idea of how the world should be, instead meeting it simply as it is. It encourages a sense of wonder, of curiosity, as though we were seeing for the very first time. It is not that the world around us changes necessarily, but rather that our experience of that world changes so fundamentally that it will never appear the same again.

Similarly, when we meet each new moment with compassion, we are released from the notion of self, no longer chasing happiness solely for our own benefit, as though there was only so much to go around, but instead motivated to bring happiness to all. Only when we focus on the happiness of others will we find happiness in our own life. It is in this spirit that we witness our relationships transforming, a deepening sense of connection, a softer, gentler approach to life.

It is my sincere wish that you enjoy this wonderful book, that it inspires and motivates, and that the words live and breathe both on the page and off the page, for the benefit of all.

Andy Puddicombe
Los Angeles, November 2015

INTRODUCTION

"Home is where I want to be
But I guess I'm already there."
TALKING HEADS

Being human can be tough. The gift of life is a miracle but it comes with complications and setbacks that many of us struggle to cope with. We know the goal is to be happy and fulfilled and there are many great examples of a "successful life" that we can compare with our own, or hold ourselves up to. There are those who appear to cruise through, seemingly having managed to get a hold of the secret "life manual"—but it doesn't take away the fact that life is challenging a lot of the time, and many of us simply don't know how to navigate our way through it. It begs the question—what *is* a successful life? Is it incremental? So that at the end of your days you can sit and calculate the great times vs. the bad times and see if you passed the test? What is life supposed to be? How on earth do we know if our life is going well?

The trouble is that when you ask one question, it just seems to beget another.

I have been working on a one-to-one basis with people for almost 30 years, first as a psychotherapist and then as a Five-Element acupuncturist; and it is in the nature of what I do that I come into contact with many people who are in trouble in some way. They may have suffered a trauma, a relationship breakdown or serious illness; or they may, after years of striving, simply have got to a point where their lives feel somehow empty and meaningless. Perhaps my job gives me a slightly colored view of the world, but I don't think so. Those life cruisers, with the manual? They, too, tend to run into problems at some point, the shiny veneer having concealed bottled-up worries which, like water finding its way through a tiny crack in a rock, will eventually manifest themselves, either as psychological difficulties or in the form of physical disease.

In our fast-paced, aspirational culture it's accepted as normal for us to look endlessly outside ourselves for meaning and purpose—what can I get? Where will I be? In early life we look to our parents as role models; but as we, and they, get older, we realize that they don't really have the answers—nor do our friends or the names in lights that we're meant to look up to. In the meantime, we plunge ourselves into work, tasks and routines, our relationships, social life, hobbies—almost anything as we look for ourselves.

Of course, we all want to do well, to get on. But all

this looking ahead has the effect of keeping us in the thrall of a perpetual future: "I just need to get away on holiday"; "when the kids have left home, when we've paid off the mortgage, we can really start enjoying ourselves"; "if only we didn't have this rain." And yet the truth is that when we do eventually get there, there's rarely any real sense of arrival, there are no flags—and, even if there are, the celebration's all too often short-lived as we jump to focus on "the next best thing." If we're not looking forward all the time, we're lamenting or feeding off the past—either in the form of nostalgia or of regrets—that bad love affair, the day we got sacked, or were tricked into that deal that lost us so much money . . .

So, let me ask you: how often do you stop, and look inward and find yourself content with what's here and now? And how often do you hear someone else doing that: simply relishing the joy of the now?

Many people in the world today equate happiness with being busy or even mildly stressed; they say it makes them feel "alive." But as we shall see, this thought is just part of a whole range of problems caused by how disconnected we have become from our true selves.

*We put our faith and trust in the illusory future, and don't seem to wake up to the fact that this limited "reality" isn't the full picture and inevitably just doesn't deliver: that **what we're looking for simply isn't out there***.

All in the mind

Our ability to think, to rationalize and judge is, we believe, our greatest gift as human beings; it is what defines us, and sets us apart from the rest of the animal kingdom.

When, in the 17th century, the French philosopher Descartes declared, "I think, therefore I am," this was deemed cause for mighty celebration. Here was enlightenment. We took his wisdom on board as a mantra for life, brushing aside in one fell swoop thousands of years of ancient wisdom.

But, as I have said, this very Western idea of the soul residing in our thinking minds is also at the root of our contemporary malaise. It shifted our point of perception from a mystical and spiritual perspective to the perspective of logic and judgment, and ever since then we've been trapped within the limitations of the mind, caught in a dualistic reality of this or that, good or bad, right or wrong.

Standing in the place of "I think" limits us in time and space and for many people causes great suffering and pain. I will be looking at the dangers of excessive rationalism in the next few chapters, but for now, consider the opposite:

*I **am**, therefore I think.*

Throwing off the blinkers and stepping back to stand in the place of "I am" gives us a whole new, open perspective—and sense of freedom. It enables us to stop being lost in our thoughts, and instead to *observe* what we think.

That there is a great deal of unhappiness in people today is not, in my view, because anything specific is wrong, but because we've forgotten how to retreat from our thinking minds and take pleasure in the bliss of simply being alive—to "be"; and to know that one's existence is so much more than a mere sequence of events that plays out before us, confirming we're "somebody" with a "life."

Our ability to think can, of course, be a wonderful tool. But that is all it is: a tool, one which needs to be used well.

We have ended up living almost exclusively "in the head." And the truth is that, despite all our brilliant cultural and technical contributions, all the benefit of our experience, and a whole lot of idealism and good will, we human beings have not wholly succeeded in our bid to create a perfect world.

We have toiled and achieved and striven for control, often doing untold damage to the planet—and ourselves—in the process. As the environmentalist David Suzuki said, "We're in a giant car heading towards a brick wall and everyone's arguing over where they're going to sit."

The call of home

Do you remember being lost as a child in the supermarket? In among the dog food and illegible yellow signs—it can feel very scary. Phew, we think. Thank God for being grown up. We no longer have to experience that terrible panicked feeling, of running around and trying to find our way back to safety.

And yet, even as supposedly mature adults, something of that feeling remains, doesn't it? A niggling voice that is never quite silenced. We may know our way home these days, as in back to the place where we reside and keep our possessions.

But somehow this is not quite enough. Because the "home" we're really looking for is beyond our current perception, and this homing instinct that compels us to return has all too often become confused with external pursuits and acquisitions.

Buffeted as we are by the noise and vicissitudes of everyday life, we lose the ability to tap into our inner selves. And then, before we know it, we have become so distracted—we have traveled so far from "home"—that we don't even know we're lost anymore.

> *"A few times in my life I've had moments of absolute clarity. When for a few brief seconds the silence drowns out the noise and I can feel rather than think, and things seem so sharp*

and the world seems so fresh. It's as though it had all just come into existence.

"I can never make these moments last. I cling to them, but like everything, they fade. I have lived my life on these moments. They pull me back to the present, and I realize that everything is exactly the way it was meant to be."

CHRISTOPHER ISHERWOOD

I imagine these brief moments of clarity that Isherwood talks of as glimpses of being "at home." Though fleeting, their very presence is enough for him to know that the world he inhabits has a natural flow that is permanently okay; to use his language, "the way it was meant to be."

I am going to be talking a lot about "home" in this book, "home" as in true peace, the permanent place inside yourself where you are always okay. Believe me, it is by no means out of reach. You just need to take the steps to get back there.

Everything you need you have

Many of you reading this book will have come to it because you believe or suspect there is something not right about you or your life. What it will reveal to you may therefore come as a surprise, for it will show you that there is nothing intrinsically wrong with you. This book is not so much about learning something new or finding a new strategy to cope with life. The aim is rather to show you how to look at things from a different perspective, and help you uncover this truth:

Everything you need to be happy and well, you already have inside. Once you have located this reality within—and live from this place—the change that occurs is both natural and effortless.

When I started out as a therapist I thought I had to "do" something. For a long time I searched outside myself for answers; I traveled the world, I trained and worked, and maintained a meditation practice and spent thousands of hours reading, studying and learning from the people who came to me for help.

And then one day the penny dropped, and I realized that as long as there is an atmosphere of love and trust in the treatment room, then miraculously, there is nothing more for me to "do" than be present. As one of my most important teachers once said to me, "Invite them to join you at 'home'—and they will be at home themselves."

There is a certain ritual about a patient arriving in the treatment room. They sit down, give themselves permission to *be* themselves and most importantly know that in this space they're free. In these conditions, the prob-

GERAD KITE

lems they have brought to the room can quickly lose their hold, as their attention moves somewhere else. Whereas they may have been entirely preoccupied by their physical and emotional pain, within a very short time the focus can be shifted to a peaceful, pain-free, loving place. And suddenly they are very much at "home"—home as in the place where they are most truly themselves.

This is my unspoken invitation to you, the reader—to let me show you that there *is* another way to "be" in the world.

What I am offering is a road map home—a ten-step program which brings together what I have learned during three decades of therapeutic practice, and elements from my own personal experience of finding the path to "calm."

To help you find the route home—to the inner "you," the one behind the mask, behind the personality that you project out onto the world—I will be introducing you to a magical transformational tool, the pendulum.

The pendulum contains the power to shift our attention from the chaos of our thoughts and actions, back to our humanity—a place of contentment and peace. It teaches us about Natural Law: that no matter what transpires in life; no matter how hard we find our life to be, within all of us there is a point of balance that is permanent, peaceful, and silent—and this is our natural state.

I will be introducing you to some of the key teachings

of ancient Chinese philosophy including the Law of Five Elements; I will also, in a general way, be drawing on ideas from Christianity and other spiritual teachings. But I'd like to point out that there is nothing in this book that comes with any particular religious agenda. The great spiritual traditions may manifest themselves in different forms, but they are built on the same guiding principles—and stem from one essential root source.

As we start our journey together, the first step is to admit you're lost, and to wake up to the fact that what you consider to be freedom is largely an illusion, that you've been living in an illusory world, the world of the mind.

Wanting things to be a certain way is not freedom.
Achieving what you set out to do is not freedom.
Being the person you want to be is not freedom.

This admission takes great humility as I'm sure you've put an enormous amount of energy and time into trying to work it all out and get your life on track. In some ways, this is, yes, an "awakening"—what is known in spiritual circles as the "Direct Path"—a spontaneous awakening or enlightenment. And of course, this is not something we can just achieve by waving some magic wand.

For an epiphany of any sort to happen, most of us need a jolt such as a medical emergency or some kind of trauma—or at least some very persistent prodding. Our conditioning and all the years of brainwashing and habit-building have locked us into our minds to such a degree that we now believe everything we think. So we'll have to take the scenic route and enjoy the view along the way.

Would you like to go home? If so—let's begin.

NOTES ON READING THE BOOK

From this point on (for clarity and emphasis), I have chosen at times to capitalize certain words (e.g. Home, Self, Love, Know) when they relate exclusively to the experience of being at "Home" vs. the thoughts and activities we know in our daily lives. This difference in focus will become clearer as we proceed.

THE JOURNEY BEGINS

The Pendulum

*"Your emotions are the slaves to your thoughts,
and you are the slave to your emotions."*
ELIZABETH GILBERT

In this chapter you will become acquainted with the workings and wisdom of the pendulum, how to use it to gain insight and self-knowledge, and most importantly how to use it to transcend your current position of forever looking outside yourself for Peace.

Picture a pendulum. What you see is a weight swinging from side to side, trying to find a still resting point, or position of equilibrium, in the middle. All your attention is drawn to this movement.

If you were to refocus, however, and instead look up at the top of the pendulum shaft, you would see that here there is no movement at all: it is a fixed point.

Now imagine the pendulum as an illustration of your emotional life, where the weight or "bob" at the bottom end represents the world of the mind and its natural movement mirrors your thoughts and feelings. For our purposes, all swings of the weight to the right represent the "high" (joy/euphoria/jubilation), and all swings to the left represent the "low" (sadness/anger/depression); the midpoint between the high and the low, where the bob will eventually come to rest, is the domain of relative "calm."

I say *relative* "calm" because, while the bob at the bottom of the pendulum will eventually come to a resting point in the middle, it is nonetheless always vulnerable to influences that can move it. It is only as we move up the shaft of the pendulum that the swings become gradually less volatile until, finally, at the pivot, there is absolute stillness.

The pendulum's secret

I'd like at this point to share with you the personal circumstances that led to my discovery of the pendulum's power, and how it transformed my life—and could transform yours too.

Some time ago, a surprise stress-related illness put me in the hospital with a debilitating inflammatory disease. I went from running a busy practice to having little else to do other than stare at the ceiling. A few miles from my hospital bed, the clinic I had established was collapsing like a house of cards, my dearest friend and housemate was dying of cancer and I was at my wits' end. It was mental and physical agony. I had nowhere to run, my mind was terrorizing me night and day and that is when in a moment of desperation I remembered the pendulum.

I had been using the pendulum as a therapeutic tool on myself for years; I had also introduced it to hundreds of people as a means of gaining awareness and promoting balance. It was only now, though, that I began to grasp its other hidden dimension.

Lying there in that hospital room, I put all my faith in it, diligently observing my mind cling to the bob as it swung chaotically back and forth from high to low, low to high, and doing all I could to steer my way back to the center and the calm. It felt impossible to land, and so eventually I gave up and surrendered to the interminable swings—the rhythm of my mind.

With the image of my broken mind and body clinging to the base of the pendulum, it dawned on me that if I wanted to escape the pain I was in, the only way out was "up"—that if I started to climb the pendulum shaft I would naturally move away from the extreme and dramatic swings at the base and eventually reach the stillness at the top. It was suddenly so obvious—the further up the pendulum shaft you go, the fewer the swings you feel.

This revelation felt profound but I still wasn't sure how to make the ascent. I then realized that the pendulum was not just a balancing tool. It was a vehicle to transcend the mind and body, and that this "awareness" alone—this distraction from my current misery—was the first step. As I took this first step, the second emerged and, like a slow-moving escalator that reveals its steps one by one, so too did the pendulum offer up the steps that would lead me, like a "stairway to heaven," to the freedom of the pivot at the top. I was now able to "observe" my painful body and tortured mind as if from outside, rather than feel lost and controlled by them. I was "at peace" and could, from this calm and detached perspective, observe every thought and feeling with objectivity and compassion.

Previously I had believed that peace could only be achieved through the resolution of chaos—but now I knew that here at "Home," Peace survives chaos. The Peace I had been searching for was inside me all along.

With the pendulum as your guide, you will climb the ten steps, and finally see the mirage on the horizon for the illusion that it is. You will come to know that the origin of what it is to be human is limitless, an honor and a gift: and that a life lived from the absolute calm of "Home" offers a richness of experience beyond your wildest dreams.

LET'S LOOK AT some examples of how the pendulum operates within us.

Imagine that your starting point is in the "relative

calm"—imagine yourself sitting in stillness and holding on to the "bob."

A happy event occurs or you have a joyful or exciting thought and you start to swing toward the "high," and then, once this happy thought has been acknowledged and experienced, you naturally gravitate back to the midpoint. Later, maybe a friend has let you down, or perhaps you've fallen and hurt yourself—now you swing to the "low"; but again, once the experience is over, you gently return and settle back to the center.

And so it goes on, a natural movement from one balanced response to the next. This is what is known as a "safe" high or low. The swing is appropriate and manageable and within range for us to settle easily back into the calm. In extreme circumstances we may swing out to the extremes of the high or the low but because of our familiarity with the calm—our default to form is habitual and simply achieved.

The reality, however, for many of us is very different. Complications in our domestic and working lives cause us to live much of the time at the extreme ends of the pendulum. In this chaotic state we find ourselves hunting and searching for Home, erroneously being drawn to one side of the pendulum or the other. We develop preferences, more often than not favoring the high, but also, at times, favoring the low. We're all different. The "compulsive swingers" love the speed and excitement of the pendulum ride, and they rarely stop anywhere en route as they cling to the weight, swinging madly from side to side. On the flip side, there are the "home bodies," the vulnerable souls who've fallen off far too many times and tend to retreat and dig down in the safety of the calm, resisting any temptation or impulse to move.

That we are so susceptible is part of the culture that we live in. Take for example the constantly evolving political climate and economy, which are literally dependent on us living at the mercy of the pendulum's swing—a state which is essential for their success and survival. "Good" marketing or politicking works on the basis that we can be drawn to the low through a sense of need or fear and then be offered something to escape to the high. An equally successful strategy is to keep us fascinated and attached to both extremes.

I remember seeing the stark reality of this when I was visiting the US during the time immediately after the September 11 attacks on the twin towers in New York. The country was on red alert, and at the bottom of the TV screen was a permanent band of color that would change from a deep red to a pale yellow to give the viewer an indication of the level of threat that the country was facing. Whatever you were watching, a lighhearted comedy or an advert for hemorrhoid cream, the ever-present band of threat was there.

Despite our attention and responses to the program in hand, unconsciously we were lulled into a feeling of okayness and safety as the band turned vanilla, bringing a promise of temporary peace, only moments later to be catapulted back into the drama and fear of an imminent attack as it morphed into deep red.

Whoever was working at the TV station was clearly well aware of how to use these kinds of visually manipulative tools to keep us dependent and lost. The trouble is that the longer we are kept away from the calm, at the extreme polarities of the pendulum—the harder it is for us to climb the pendulum shaft. Those who trade in products, services or political ideologies do all they can to keep us from the Peace of the calm. They fear this place, as they cannot reach us in it: here we're safe and self-sufficient and they know this well—"you can't please a pleased"—and so almost everything around us is designed to keep us swinging back and forth.

The teaching of the pendulum is simple. We have choice. We can either live solely from the weight of our minds at the base, a victimized state where we are vulnerable to both internal and external influences that can rock us and send us swinging all over the place; or we can choose to live from the place of "Absolute Calm" at the top.

What my journey taught me was that the process of

coming "Home" requires a practical approach as well as a direct experience of what Truth is, and it is this that I would like to share with you in this book.

There are many excellent texts that espouse the beauty of the human spirit, the joy of living in the "now," the power of prayer and being mindful, but from my experience people can end up feeling even more alienated if they fail in their quest, and the destination just ends up feeling unobtainable.

The secret of the pendulum is that it can promote a profound awareness of where you are in yourself at any time. As you move up the steps, your awareness increases and, like any learning process, each step will inform the next and give texture and relief. The experience as a whole will lead to a significant shift in your primary point of perception—and this is the key to freedom.

Where are you right now? Are you gently swinging in the calm and enjoying the day? Are you perhaps clinging to the bob, tipped to the low and consumed with worry and depressing thoughts? Or, on the contrary, is your heart racing with excitement, the pendulum cranked to the high as you look forward to your upcoming summer break, a new job opportunity, a new lover? Becoming aware of where you are is your preparation for the journey and as you work through the steps (still noticing your swings) and discover the numerous levels and the variety of movements available to you—you'll

become a confident and savvy rider of the swings of the pen-
dulum and clearer when you settle in the calm.

Climbing the pendulum means gaining access to all areas; exploring its range is to become aware of the vastness of who you are, as you develop the flexibility and agility to move at will. I'll get you to a place where you'll be free to join the "compulsive swingers," to go play and have fun and ride the pendulum at the base, even though it's risky, in the knowledge that you are free because in your Self you haven't lost sight of Home. You'll even be able to indulge your morbidity as you watch the news— you'll be able to empathize, act on what you see, shored up by the knowledge that you are watching it from the safety of Home.

We all of us spend an enormous amount of time and energy seeking happiness in our lives. And we feel cheated when it eludes us or when it seems to go as fast as it comes; but that is its nature—

Happiness is not a permanent state. The permanent state ex-
ists within, and is the cause of all things. This is the Truth of
who you are.

So come—join me. Climb the steps of the pendulum and experience a life lived from Peace.

Once you're at Home, which is permanent, still and un-changing, you'll be more comfortable and at ease with the world that changes. When we reside within the calm, in the zone of "Home," we're directly connected and in touch with a more expansive reality where we know that everything we need is already here. We Know who we are, and in this safe place our sense of "Being" is peaceful, undemanding and most importantly—enough. We are content.

The steps

Think of taking each of the steps as like peeling away the layers from an onion as we make our way up to the top—shedding as we go. Step 1 starts by looking at our "outer skin," our most outer life, created by the self that identifies as an individual through the mind; by Step 10, we've discarded the layers of our "thinking world" and have reached the subtlest level of our existence, our in-ner "life"—the sweet core of Home.

The early steps are all about developing "awareness." Awareness is the key to finding your way Home and in-volves a degree of rehearsal and practice as many of us are not in the habit of being aware of anything outside our normal habits and routines. The first five steps are here to rekindle a natural curiosity in you as you make your journey inward.

Steps 6–7 are the domain of form (body) where you shift your attention away from your mind and emotions and develop a greater awareness of your physical form. When you operate from your body you are bound by natural laws, which feed through to the mind and regulate your thoughts. These two steps have a more limited pendulum swing due to their closer proximity to the pivot at the top, and act as a bridge between the complexity of the World of Mind below and the simplicity of Home and the Self above.

Steps 8–10 are, respectively, the approach, the threshold and inner space of Home. Here your attention is beyond your body and your mind and you uncover the permanent Peace that exists within. The swing of the pendulum as you take these final and pivotal steps is minimal and then negligible. You are now beyond the dualistic world of your mind: Peace and stillness define your world.

Each of the ten steps provides an opportunity for you to review and get to know every aspect of yourself—a process which will in itself "lighten" the load.

I'd also like to highlight two areas of activity that will help you on your way.

How to develop your inner GPS

Create a habit of knowing where you are on the pendulum. Imagine where you are right now. Ask yourself

throughout the day, "How am I?" and observe your movement—or lack of movement—on the pendulum swing.
Is there a particular area where you seem to land con-
sistently? Do you naturally come back to the calm? Are
you constantly striving for the high? What stops you from
settling?

True Rest

True Rest is the name given to any activity, thought or
action that brings you Home to the calm. Trying to climb
the steps when your pendulum is swinging back and forth
is difficult and counterproductive so True Rest will help
you steer a steady course. True Rest is not prescriptive. It
is very personal; it might be something that you already
know can help to settle you inside, or you might need to
go out and find it.

For example, True Rest for me is walking the dogs,
swimming, meditating, watching German TV (I enjoy
languages) or cooking. These activities have the effect of
shifting my attention away from busy, chaotic thoughts
and give me a chance to tune into the calm inside.

When I consult the pendulum and realize that I have
been too high, too low or swinging madly, I realize it's
time for True Rest and a return to Home. The beauty and

elegance of the pendulum is that the further up the pendulum you go, the less the swings. Consequently, there's much greater leeway, as the repercussions are not so extreme.

Another example: if you're feeling very sad and stuck in the low at the base of the pendulum shaft, going out and getting drunk can be very destructive. However if you've already made your way, let's say, halfway up it, your sadness will be less potent and the bottle of red wine will have less power to cause a pendulum swing and so any damage is naturally controlled.

For those of you who have reached the top of the pendulum and live from Peace, you will probably find that you no longer want to turn to drinking to change your state or, if you do drink, it's a celebration of being at Home and more than likely you will imbibe less.

One of the greatest bonuses of climbing up the steps is that each step is a form of "true rest" in itself. The pendulum and what it teaches us is cumulative, so the way Home becomes easier and easier with each step you take.

Make a list of the activities you know will bring you back to midpoint. Keep it on you to remind you of what you can do when you know you've left the calm.

CASE STUDY—GRAHAM

I knew Graham long before he came to me as a patient so I was very aware of how he struggled in the world. He could be a delightfully open, friendly and loving character, but he was also tricky and contrary. He was highly intelligent and could run circles around you if you challenged him.

At the point that he came to me for help he was in a terrible state. He had alienated almost everyone he knew and was at a loss to know what to do with his life, spending most of the day huddled in the corner of his room, drinking and smoking marijuana.

Our sessions to begin with were permeated with hate—Graham's hatred of all sorts of things that he had become fixated on. He hated the opera, for many reasons, but mostly because "rich people" would congregate there. He would obsess about the faults and ills of this particular seam of society. He hated bankers too. Anyone who, in his view, had more than their fair share. Indeed Graham resented other people's apparent happiness and success to a sometimes alarming degree. He looked at the world through a paranoid lens and only saw a place he couldn't join.

I spent much of the time trying to get him to see that what other people seemed to have, or not have, was irrelevant to his personal journey in life. But it was not easy to reach him. And, as our sessions continued, I came to understand how he had come to be in this painful, suspicious state.

Born and brought up in Texas, he had been bullied from infancy by an overbearing, sometimes violent father. He had learned as a boy that the world was a mean, destructive place, a place without rationality or justice.

The idea of the pendulum fascinated him. He'd love to "play the pendulum," as he called it, but said he couldn't see it helping him, as he already knew where he would reside on it: at the extreme of either the high or the low. His identity was that of either dark passion or cold indifference and he despised mediocrity. The idea of the midpoint or the calm of the pendulum was, he said, abhorrent to him.

I gave Graham homework in the form of a diagram of the pendulum and asked him to put a mark on the curve each day to record how he felt. After the first week of charting his emotional state, he came back with an interesting observation—and complaint. He complained that as each day passed and his misery increased he was frustrated that the limitations of the pendulum had limited his expression. Having already put himself at the extreme end of the "low" when he left me, he'd found there was nowhere else to go in spite of his increasing wretchedness.

"So what did you do?" I naively asked.

"I stole a bottle of wine," he answered, grinning. We looked at his chart and the theft had scored him enough points to swing to the "high." Misery had transformed itself into excitement.

"What happened then?" I asked.

"I got drunk and don't remember much else." And so, now here we were back in the extreme of the low— and no doubt in the process of cooking up enough energy to burst back into the next big high.

As we sat in silence digesting this, I noticed a change in Graham. He softened, looking at me, and placed a finger on the calm of the drawing of the pendulum before us and asked, "Why would anyone want to be there?"

Graham prided himself on being in control; control of his depression and misery, control of his outrageous behavior. But now looking at himself from the perspective of the pendulum, he realized these enormous swings were simply his nature following natural laws. They were what he did—the outward manifestation of a mood or thought at a particular time, in a particular place—but they had little to do with *him*.

"What goes up must come down," he mimicked and laughed.

Seeing that his behavior was not entirely of his own making was enough to confound Graham's thinking.

He now knew that he had little control over his wild outbursts but that, in spite of his troubled life and the resultant patterns of unmanageable behavior, "he" was okay.

Graham continues to struggle to this day. How could he not? To have his world shattered through violence at such a tender age has left an indelible mark on his perception of himself and the world. But through the power of the pendulum to direct him Home, he is more able to find a way to be calm; because, like me when I recognized the gift of the pendulum that day in my hospital bed, he knows in his heart that inner Peace is untouchable and intact and survives all the chaos outside.

The pendulum is a great visual tool to occupy your mind and focus you as you make the journey home. So, if it helps you, make your own.

Take a small square piece of cardboard that will fit in a small bag or a pocket, and in the bottom left-hand corner write "LOW," and in the bottom right-hand corner write "HIGH"—and at the midpoint between those two words, write "CALM."

Now, with another piece of cardboard, cut out the shape of a pendulum shaft that will fit onto the card you have already prepared. Punch a hole at the top of the pendulum and also at the top of the square piece of card and join them with a butterfly clip. You now have your pendulum that can swing from side to side on top of the card below and you can chart your emotional state at any time.

Your pendulum is your new best friend. It is loyal and honest and will tell you many things about your Self. It has the power of reflection, to tell you when you're out of control, it will warn you when you need to take a break and it will even alert you to the need to spice it up a bit and have some fun. Most importantly it will let you know when you have left the "calm."

By regularly using the pendulum you will develop a habit of "stepping back" from your thoughts and emotions and looking objectively at what's going on inside you. This reflex to retreat from the madness of your thoughts and feelings gives you perspective and a breathing point where you can pause.

One of the greatest gifts of the pendulum comes when you follow its "rule," which is that **choices or decisions must only be made when you are in the safety of the "calm."**

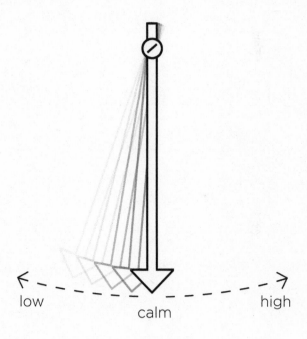

low   high

calm

THE WORLD OF MIND

Awareness

"Who do you think you are?"
THE SPICE GIRLS

The World of Mind contains five steps. The first four are designed to give you objectivity on how you see yourself, to help you watch your mind at work and how it shapes your world. At this early stage, curiosity is the key.

In Step 1, I want you simply to become aware of how you are. We begin by examining the mind's pièce de résistance—its first thought, "I," and how the power of this little word can keep us trapped in a two-dimensional world. In Step 2 we'll explore the games our mind loves to play and in Step 3 we'll see how our behavior, although for the most part acquired, can define who we think we are. In Step 4 we look at ourselves in relation to others and the pitfalls of relationships when governed by our mind.

Step 5, our final step in the World of Mind, is a powerful and pivotal step on the journey Home. It shifts our perspective from a predominantly outward view, to an inner focus that promotes personal awareness and helps re-root us in "reality" (the natural world) and prepares us for the World of Body.

By being reintroduced to the true cause of the way we are, *prior* to the emergence of our mind and its labels— we will have remembered our rightful place in the Universe. We will have learned how to step back from our mind, our emotions, opinions and beliefs and realize that the depth of our existence is not out there somewhere, but found inside. We will have become the observer rather than the observed.

Know thyself

The Ancient Greek aphorism "know thyself" has had many interpretations over the centuries and for our purposes when putting a foot on the first step of the pendulum—these two powerful words are ever relevant and true: knowledge is the key. You need to "know yourself" at every step: know yourself in thought, and know yourself in action.

These first five steps of the pendulum are an acknowledgment that you *think* you're "somebody": that this singularly focused "thought" has captured your attention at the expense of the bigger picture of "You." It's all about awareness. Just as you would observe an object you've never seen before—so too now will you look at yourself as if for the first time.

For example, a good friend, Jack, defines himself as a "generous man"—and he is. But this character description is now a label and in spite of it being a lovely trait—it has become a defining characteristic of his personality which he has to maintain and keep alive. He's trapped himself (by his own admission) as he often feels used and wants to tell everyone to "go to hell"—instead he just keeps smiling and giving.

Here's your starting point on the way Home—to take the opportunity to examine yourself (privately) and question who you really are objectively and without judgment. What are your personal labels, do you think? Be ruthlessly honest with yourself and put it all out on the table—warts 'n' all.

"I am here
I am here, now.
I have always been here, always."
EDMUND J. LADD

Every time we identify ourselves through our mind we use the word "I." But who is this "I"? How do we know the difference between the "I" which is the personality we project to the outside world, and the inner "I," the "Self" which exists at some deeper level that is more difficult to explain?

What does individual identity really mean and how is it that the "freedom" we associate with "I" leaves many of us feeling somehow incomplete and lost?

More than likely the last time you were truly free was soon after your birth and in the few years before you realized that the fuzzy world around you could be broken down and seen as different components, with each bit valued and labeled. In this new world everything suddenly *lost* its freedom and was burdened with a name. Even more striking was the news that you also had a name and by definition you were separate from what you had previously experienced as the blissful Oneness of Being.

As infants we begin this differentiated experience of our new self by employing the word "me." "Me wants to eat," or "Me is tired," as we instinctively resist the formidable weight of the "I" word being placed on us.

As we grow up in the culture of "I," the primary message we are given is that we are all separate from each other—"individuals"—and that our existence is totally dependent on the many labels that we as individuals must create and maintain for ourselves: positive and negative, good and bad.

I was recently with an old friend who asked me what this book was about.

"The book is saying that the ultimate truth of who you are is not the same as who you 'think' you are," I said.

"Oh," she said, back like a dart. "You mean all the labels—like 'I'm a mother,' 'I teach little kids,' 'I like spicy food, etc.'"

"Spot on. You see it's so simple."

And then she paused and said, "But if we take all the labels away—what's left? Surely, the labels are who we are—we are nothing without them."

Her 11-year-old son Oscar was also present and so I thought I would try and find out how a child, having more recently resided in the bliss of "Home," would answer the same question. "If I took away all the things you know about me, and I took away all the things I know about you—what would be left?" I asked him.

"Just the person," he said. "We'd just be two people—the same, I guess."

"Out of the mouth of babes" we hear the truth, and yet our cult—the cult of "I"—ignores their innocent voices and instead leads us to distrust their instinctive understanding about the Truth of Self as mere signs of immaturity. So committed do we become to the cult, and the relative identity conferred by what we are thinking or what our state of mind is at any one time, that we convince the "babes" they're wrong and try to show them the right and proper path. It's not long before they, too, are signed-up lifetime members—agents for the cause.

The problem starts with the illusion of freedom that comes from our thinking minds. None of us likes to think we're not free and so we collude with each other and reinforce the illusion that we are free—free to think whatever we want. This keeps us feeling safe. So we encourage each other to be independent thinkers and to be innovative and original and this uniqueness of expression continually reinforces the illusion of freedom. Before we know it we are trapped by our own brilliance.

The poor mind is overworked and overvalued—it has been given a position it doesn't want or deserve. The mind is born of the Self and is there to serve the Self to bring it to life; it is not meant to go it alone and masquerade as the Self—and yet this is what we've asked it to do. What's happened in our culture is that in the absence of

Knowing our Self, the mind has been given the position of king. The mind is now the part of us that says "I": "I'm the one! I'm the Creator! I'm in control!" Yet it has no idea really what it's meant to do. It is out of its depth, and floundering: and in the absence of "Knowing" the Truth, it starts to make things up, often with devastating outcomes. Better that than a scary void.

Sometimes mind control can make us feel very good. "You're amazing," it says, for no other reason than—why not? Alternatively your mind might tell you "You're a bad person and you'll never succeed," a lecture that could be based on little more than a random scan of current circumstances and memory. Yet we believe it all so much that we live our lives from this place. We even take our minds to therapy and try to understand why our thoughts and feelings are telling us these things. And sometimes it gets even worse. In our search for real meaning and understanding of our self, we end up constructing a whole new layer of narrative, foraging around for evidence that either confirms or denies the message being delivered by our mind.

There's nothing wrong with a cult. It is what it is—it's a cult, by which I mean a group belief system ruled by the mind, the culture we've created and collectively choose to live within. But what we need to realize is that this "I," the origin of the mind, is a construct, and only a small part of a greater Truth, and as easily as we can create it, we can also deconstruct all that we have built and see the wonder of what's left behind. As Oscar pointed out—when all the labels have been taken away everyone is just "a person" and at core we're all the same.

CASE STUDY—KITTY

Like all of my patients, Kitty arrives in my treatment room with many labels. She's an attractive, highly educated woman in her late 30s, a successful lawyer. She lives with her partner Mike, and she is now ready for a child. She bursts into my treatment room full of anxiety and thrusts a handful of cash at me like a drug-crazed addict looking for a fix. She has come to me for help in getting pregnant but reels off a list of difficult and worrying things that make her feel bad. It's a maze of misery and she can't find her way out.

One session, shortly into her treatment, it dawns on me that in spite of the terrible stories—the "person" in front of me is fine. The storyteller is in good shape—it's just the stories she tells that are horrible. I decide to ask her how she's feeling, as the bearer of all this bad news.

"I feel terrible of course—my life is a mess," she replies.

I try again. "Kitty, I am asking how 'You' are right

now." Suddenly, it's as if she has woken up. "I guess I'm okay," she says, with a smile. "I'm okay. It's just everything that's going on . . ."

This moment is so innocent and simple; it feels almost like an epiphany. For a split second Kitty remembers that in spite of all the tales of her "terrible life"—when she steps back and looks inside—she's okay.

"I always run into trouble when I 'think' I'm somebody."
WREN WINFIELD

We all think we're somebody. Of course we do. After all, we all have a name—a past and a future, and events and objects we call "my life." But as you begin to take this first step on your journey, you'll begin to see that who you are is not just a collection of thoughts, memories and dreams of a future, but also the "You" that exists at a deeper level of reality and who sits quietly and peacefully "at Home" watching the story of life unfold.

Briefly shifting Kitty's attention from the mind-made misery of her "life" to the okay-ness of "Home" was a miracle—but we're all vulnerable and we easily default back to form. Kitty had the momentary experience of shifting her attention from who she thinks she is—to the One at Home who "Is." But it was short-lived and it would take some considerable time for her to finally see through the "story" of her mind, and its labels—our cult's programming is fierce.

Finding your way back Home is not only about finding freedom and peace, but a way to help understand your confused identity and the inevitable suffering that brings. You will come to realize that from this suffering an opportunity arises—the rediscovery of the Truth of who you really are prior to the emergence of "I."

We live in a culture in which the distraction and promotion of separateness and individuality are rife. And we buy into it wholesale. Let's not forget why we have started out on this journey together. The goal is not to judge or change anything that the mind creates. Instead, it is for you to have the ability and agility to step back from the mental drama of your life and observe your Self from the safety and permanence of Home.

When we turn away from the light of "Home," a shadow appears—which we mistake for our Self, and label "I."

There is nothing right or wrong about the "I." There's no need to demonize it or put all your attention on it, but just see it for what it is and know it's a shadow and not the light. Our problems begin when we only know and see the shadow and forget the light. But it is the light that gives birth to the shadow and not the other way around.

Surely endlessly following your shadow as you search for light is a bit daft and quite exhausting. Can you give up the chase?

Stay with me and I'll show you how.

Sleepwalking

When we live within our cult we think we're awake—but in the truest sense of this word we're not. We're as good as sleepwalking; just proceeding blindly through our daily existence and for the most part moving around our largely habitual lives using stale memories as props and signposts, rather than taking in each moment as fresh and new. It's not that different from the way we employ our mind to remember how to find the toilet in the middle of the night, eyes half shut, and even in the pitch-black.

On the morning of my 40th birthday I was in northern India with a friend. I invited him to join me and climb to the top of a hill to see a magnificent view at sunrise. On reaching the top I exclaimed, "Look at that!" "What?" my friend inquired, as he took another look and added, "But we saw this yesterday."

This moment was enlightening. The "tick—done that!" mental attitude he displayed brought home to me the folly of living from the mind. The mind is not concerned with the bigger picture of a rich and vibrant, moment by moment, sensory experience—it serves its own integrity and survival.

Think of how our sensory experiences are diluted by the mind. Half the time we no longer see, smell, taste, hear or feel. For example—cities around the world are full of smells, often deeply unpleasant ones, and yet we can walk through our home cities and smell absolutely nothing. We get onto a busy underground train, stuffed with people's odors, their manufactured fragrances, their "morning breath" and everything else—and yet, we rarely smell anything. We are people lost in dreamworlds, headphones hammering at our ears, having switched off from reality to find safety and comfort in a private and limited world.

Likewise, we're emotionally calloused and numb to the full extent of our fellow human's suffering, conditioned to walk with ease past those in need, habituated to watching the horrors of the world from the comfort of a cozy sofa, and even disguising the depth of our own feelings with robotic turns of phrase and platitudes stored in the mental software.

The natural state of "Being"—to be present to each and every moment—has been lost as our attention has shifted away from the freshness of the present and fixated on our memories of the past and the fantasy of future hopes and dreams. We're lost in our minds; we've strayed far from Home.

The drive for success

One of the greatest traps set by our culture is our obsession with the idea of success. Many of the teenagers I see in my practice are bound and chained by the need to succeed. Success is offered by their parents, even the most well-meaning ones, as both a carrot and a whip.

This in itself would not be so bad if the idea was limited to passing exams and having good manners and social skills, but the idea of success permeates almost every thought and action. We can all identify with this. It's part of the conditioning, the need to be in control.

When I was in my early 20s I opened a small business that ran for just over two years. It was moderately successful but felt overwhelming and afforded me little time to "hang out" and socialize with my peers. As my interest waned the business started to fail and eventually closed down. At the time I was aware that it had come to a natural end as it did not serve me and therefore it was appropriate to let it close. I didn't mind. However, in the eyes of my peers, it had gone wrong and I had failed.

I moved to the States shortly afterward, much chastened.

Standing in a supermarket checkout queue one day, I started chatting with a man about where I was from and why I had moved. I told him my "failed business" story, to which he replied, "That's great! Once you've gone bust two more times, then you'll know what you're doing!" This different perspective flipped my thinking completely—suddenly the demise of my business was relabeled as a success and a useful part of my education.

In the West we have a relatively fixed idea of success or failure, which is unyielding and restrictive. When I first started treating patients for all kinds of symptoms I was also sucked into this success/fail paradigm, which was exciting when treatment resulted in a symptom vanishing and dispiriting when it didn't. I quickly realized that this pressure—and my own emotional investment in success—did not serve my patients or me. My expectations only created more pressure for them.

Brian, a patient I saw many years ago, was a wonderful teacher for me. His idea of "success" dominated and controlled him until one day his life started cracking up, and in the process he found his Self.

On our first meeting he seemed most keen to talk about a recent skiing injury. It was only later that it emerged he wanted help because he was "firing blanks." The cause of his infertility was unknown but he was determined to father his own child. The impact of his diagnosis had been devastating for him. He felt emasculated

GERAD KITE

and talked a great deal about his shame and damaged pride. His wife was extremely supportive and understanding but she was keen to move forward with assisted fertility treatment using her own eggs—and donor sperm. For Brian the thought of his wife carrying another man's child was unacceptable and incredibly painful. He went through the emotions of someone whose partner was considering adultery, which deepened his sense of isolation and anger.

Treatment was a long and very painful process for Brian. But once he'd reluctantly accepted his wife's request that they try and conceive using donor sperm, we both agreed that our sessions were more about him accepting the possibility of raising a child that was not genetically his own, than about improving his fertility. Many of the conversations we had were around his fixed idea of what a successful life is and how things *should* be. Having never before questioned or examined his beliefs it was a revelation to him that this intense period of suffering had somehow opened the door to the possibility that he could choose to "change his mind" and think differently.

Quite soon, he developed an understanding and vocabulary about himself which I doubt he would ever have imagined possible. The issues were not just about becoming a father but touched on his whole worldview: his sense of himself, his family, his relationships and career. Over time and after many long discussions on "breaking the rules," Brian woke up and rebelled against his mind by openheartedly accepting what was happening around him, and by the time his son was born it was clear he'd found his way Home.

Living life within the cult and viewing the world from the mind's "I" limits the view and your depth of perspective. By stepping back and realizing there is a broader and less final point of view you'll know the journey Home has begun.

"Success is not final, failure is not fatal: it is the courage to continue that counts." WINSTON S. CHURCHILL

"Success" is an idea and is subjective. It's just another way for the "I" to judge and label and complicate the simplicity of your unfolding life. Living life from Home is gentler than this. There is no longer such a thing as "success"—just events playing out, finding their way, following Natural Law.

*"I was going to change my clothes, but I changed
my mind instead."*
JAROD KINTZ

We all play mind games. We play them because we can, and because that's what a mind does—it loves to play and it makes stuff up. In this "secret place" we can think whatever we like and we can create fantasies and stir up memories at will.

The mind is an ingenious "game box" that can create, store, absorb, calculate, edit, project, in short "do" almost anything. The problem, as we have seen, is that we have forgotten that the mind is a tool and let it become our God; while its true role is to serve "us," this dynamic has been flipped so that we now serve "it." For many of us it has taken on the role of defining us—and we think that's all we are. We're like the dog owner who's dragged around by his pooch wondering why on earth he's so exhausted and feels so out of control.

The mind tells us that who we are is our own creation but this creates a faux sense of freedom. It's true that what we *project* from our mind is our creation but that doesn't mean it's the whole picture. For example, if

I think someone has lied to me because I heard one thing, but then someone tells me something to the contrary (and I believe this), I have now constructed a new "reality" and all my thoughts will now fall into line with this new computation. On a profound level this new piece of information will filter through to every related thought stored in my mind, just as the ripples on a pond will extend all the way to the edge.

Another example: someone lets me down in an intimate relationship—they cheat on me, and this new piece of information sends shock waves through my being, landing on every previous relationship I've had stored as memory. I now relabel every memory of intimacy and love under the new banner of betrayal and loss. "I've never really been able to trust anyone in my life," the new recording says.

We do this all the time, changing the past and recalibrating the future as we juggle our thoughts and memories and reset them to our current way of thinking.

The human mind is a brilliant and complex "machine"—but it is not fail-safe. Like the stomach that exists to digest food, and the liver that exists to process toxins, so too does our mind exist to work just like another functioning organ in the body, one which is dependent on energy to do its job. And if we are tired and resources are low, it will default to memory, an experience less energy-zapping than taking on new input and producing new pathways. Some people have been running on reserve energy for so long they are still living from the memory of ten years ago and don't even realize it. The projection is so vivid and familiar they think it's real.

Once we've created certain actions or stories that work for us—i.e. activities that produce sensations we enjoy—our mind will naturally default back to these for familiarity's sake and as a husbanding of resources. This is what we know as habits or, at the extreme end, addiction. And essentially it is about the mind laying down patterns that are familiar and therefore compelling.

For example, when you walk down your own familiar street it's likely that little will have changed since you last looked. Your mind, nevertheless, receives the new image and compares it to the one on file. Providing the image is much the same as before, you're more than likely to "see" the memory (the one that's on file) rather than the subtle changes that will naturally have occurred. It really is quite clever as it means you can make it on autopilot all the way to the local store and back again using minimal energy reserves.

Let's look at it another way: we are culturally in the habit of looking forward to Friday as it's the end of the week. As we move closer to it, our mind reminds us that this illusory day (because of course there's no such *thing* as Friday; it is merely another label) is looming and our programming tells us it's "a good thing." The body responds to this message and produces endorphins that support the idea and we believe it even more. And then Friday arrives and there's . . . well, perhaps not much going on—the weekend is looking bare, so now what do we do? Look forward to next Friday?

Every piece of information received through the senses is logged by the mind and organized and filed, and then projected back out to the outside world. It is as if two mirrors are facing each other, one receiving the information, the other creating a reflection inside and then sending that image back out into the world on an endless loop.

When I first started practicing acupuncture I operated from a sweet little Georgian shop-front property in my local area. My father had given me a beautiful antique clock as a graduation present that I proudly hung in my little waiting room on the ground floor of the shop. I was doing well with building my patient list and was pleased as I was attracting some quite influential people who both intimidated and impressed me.

One of these patients was a well-known actor who came to me for back problems, but after only two sessions he confessed he had a more troubling "symptom"—kleptomania. He told me it was impossible for him to go anywhere without taking something from the property. It really didn't matter what it was as long as he took something with him.

"What kind of things?" I asked.

"Well, anything, really. For example I just took a pile of deposit forms from the bank." He pulled a handful of crinkled rectangles of paper from his pocket.

In my naïveté this behavioral "tic" didn't seem so very bad. "Well that's okay," I reassured him. "It's not as if you are setting out to hurt someone."

"I also stole an eraser from my best friend's child's pencil case," he added, apparently disappointed.

For the rest of that session, I continued focusing on his back as the main complaint and left the subject of his kleptomania alone.

A week later I greeted him once more, showed him into the treatment room and excused myself to wash my hands. I returned to the room to find he was gone. I went downstairs to the waiting room to see if he was there and had maybe forgotten something—but no. Puzzled, I sat down to see if he would return and then suddenly knew he would not be back—the absence of my father's gift was a strong enough clue.

The lesson for me during this formative time of my career was twofold. Just because someone appears to be "normal" or "sane" doesn't mean they are, and that when people tell you what's wrong with them—be sure to take it in.

This "mind game" (also known as kleptomania) clearly produced some kind of sensation that my patient enjoyed—so much so he'd take anything to get his fix. If we take the morality out of this story and just see it as a pattern of behavior it's easier to understand. People love the sensation of checking their Facebook account, brushing their hair, or following routines that seem quite normal on first inspection but hide a deep and ingrained habit, which, if disturbed or taken away, can create a serious dent in their well-being and even their health.

The truth is—we're all a bit crazy. For the most part we believe every thought we have and yet I'm sure that if everyone's thoughts were automatically broadcast, we'd be policing our minds all day.

An old friend of mine when viewed alone (behind closed doors) is what you might easily call "barking mad." Terrified of any disorder, or dirt in his environment, he manages to come up with all kinds of theories as to why he shouldn't do the simplest of things. For example, if his infant child is upstairs asleep, you can't turn on the kettle in the kitchen below. He doesn't advertize the reasoning behind this precaution but his sister told me that his fear is that the steam from the kettle will find its way up to the baby and burn her face. Madness? Yes—of course, but this kind of behavior is going on all over the world, all the time, in the hidden recesses of people's private lives. The upside is that my friend's amazing at his job. He is a hotel manager and his attention to detail wins him awards year on year and sets standards of care and safety that his employers would never want to change.

The 1944 film *Gaslight* ended up giving its own name to a "mind game" that is probably happening in a house near you—right now. The film tells the tale of a woman driven crazy (literally) by her new husband who convinces her of things she has done—that she hasn't. His goal is to drive her nuts, put her in a mental institution and then find her deceased mother's jewels which he believes are hidden in the house.

Quite an elaborate plot, but the sinister message of the film when it came out was accurate and disturbing enough for its title to become forever associated with this kind of mental torture.

CASE STUDY—ANDREW

My patient Andrew was being "gaslighted" but he didn't have a clue. What brought him to me was adult-onset asthma. He'd met Lucy, his partner, on a singles holiday in Antigua about ten years previously. They had a great time hanging out at night, windsurfing by day, and after a few days were really quite close. At the end of the holiday it turned out that Lucy was on the rebound. She'd recently ended a relationship with someone and was not really ready for a new relationship—or so she said. When Andrew realized this he was very disappointed but put it down to a holiday romance and moved on. About three months later (out of the blue) he got a text message from Lucy saying that she'd been thinking about him and would he like to meet up again.

At first he was excited, but he was also nervous as he hadn't stopped thinking about her since they'd met and worried it might lead to nothing again. They met and immediately clicked straight back into where they left off. That night they stayed together and after that they barely left each other's company, although they rarely met up with other people as this group dynamic seemed to produce conflict between them.

"Why do you think being with other people is a problem?" I asked. "She gets really upset if I talk to anyone," he said casually. "But why?" I persisted. "She tells me I am always talking rubbish and that I am embarrassing her and showing her up."

After a great deal of probing into his experience of the past ten years and what was going on now, it became clear that Andrew had taken on the role of inadequacy and was convinced that he had issues with women in general—that he was an "ignorant flirt." Trying to match Andrew, the man in front of me, with this label did not make sense to me, and so I questioned him further.

"Lucy says I've got problems with relating to people and she's told me what people say about me," he explained, still loyal to their story. "She says people say I'm boring and that I'm a real downer when I show up."

Andrew was confused and sad, unable to find excitement or be joyful about anything. He used all the positive words one would expect from a happy, healthy man, but the man in the room was tired, defeated and in some ways heartbroken. The drip-by-drip manipulation he'd been suffering for years had taken its toll on him and he no longer knew who he was. His relationship was making him ill.

Lucy from the outset was clearly terrified of losing Andrew and so she used the only strategy she knew: to systematically destroy his self-confidence to the point that he would operate from insecurity and doubt, so that he would end up withdrawing from life and become dependent on her.

This revelation came as a result of many weeks in couples' counseling—where they went at Andrew's request. Sadly their relationship did not survive this shift in awareness and they parted company—wiser nonetheless. When Andrew realized he had been brainwashed, he had to admit that the brilliant mind that he assumed directed his life was actually a very confused and faulty construct that did not necessarily have his best interests at heart.

The lesson here is that the mind can be an unreliable companion, and that it will easily accept an invitation from another's mind when it seems there is a match. There is nothing wrong with this—this is the dance of mind—but it does produce a great deal of unnecessary waste and suffering if our blinkered focus tells us that this dance is the only dance and we miss out on the bigger and more vibrant life experience that goes on beyond the reach of our thinking mind. A life lived from mind is not a life that is free or at peace.

Andrew's asthma improved the day he liberated himself from his signed-up role of the oppressed victim—a great example of how the body in its role as witness will let us know when we have strayed from the calm of the pendulum and lodged ourselves in either the low or the high. Andrew's ten years in the field of the low had become so familiar to him he could have stayed there for the rest of his life—some of us do—but thankfully his body alerted him to a "problem" and luckily for him he discovered the cause.

The message of this story could be told in many ways—via different characters, different scenarios and different physical symptoms. What's important to recognize is that *what we think is our only reality is in fact just a projection of our mind and produced as the circumstances of our life.* I want to urge you to avoid making a judgment on whatever situation lies before you at any given time; instead, try and see it for what it is, and rather than label it as a problem or something difficult—or even a great triumph—leave it alone, step back, and simply become aware.

The point of freedom lies where we can see everything objectively and know it for what it is. I've had many patients who have absolute clarity about the appalling situations that they choose to exist within, but they see them for what they are, and are at peace with the chaos and are fundamentally well within themselves.

For example, I have a patient called Sandra whose living situation is very difficult indeed. Her upstairs neighbors are loud, and blatantly aggressive to her—destroying her plants, leaving dog feces outside her door—yet denying it all. She's been to the police but as she is unable to provide any real evidence (the bullies are smart) there's nothing they can do to help.

When she first came to me we spent a great deal of time trying to strategize a practical solution. We talked about how she may have contributed to this frightening dynamic and even considered the primitive response of taking revenge. Sandra's mind was programmed to react to these people, to position them as her enemy and also to project on them a whole bunch of emotions that should have stayed in the vaults of memory. This was more like "mind wars" than "mind games."

Aware that the drama was ramping up and possibly heading to a very nasty end, I suggested Sandra try something new—to do nothing. I asked her to retreat from her mental battle, accept and forgive the neighbors' behavior as just "behavior," and to step back into the place in her Self where she is okay. This is of course a big ask for someone who believes she is not okay and is primed to explode.

I suggested she go home, find a comfortable space in the house, sit in a chair she enjoyed and resist the temptation to react, just listen to the quiet inside. I suggested she do this as much as possible for one week. A week later Sandra entered the room, and calmly sat down. She had taken my advice and spent almost the whole week sitting in her favorite chair sketching. She had somehow managed to find peace in a hopeless and ugly place and knew that in spite of a very difficult situation that possibly would not change, she could be safe "at Home."

From here she slowly found the courage to challenge the neighbors, assert herself with force, and even cry in front of them when it was all too much—because now she said she knew she was okay—she always was.

Free will and the illusion of freedom

One of the mind's darker games is to convince us of things that aren't true. The mind can make us feel terrible about ourselves with self-deprecating taunts; but equally it is also a great PR machine and can convince us we're happy even if we're not.

Ursula was a feted dress designer and had her own shop in London's West End. She was successful in every way. She had a poster-boy boyfriend, a glittering group of equally successful friends and she regularly featured in the "who's fab and gorgeous" sections of the press. She had it all—not to mention her dossier of symptoms.

She came to me because she had just been diagnosed with breast cancer and she was adamant that this new symptom was linked to all the others in her bulging file. "The medical professionals have been negligent," she said, "and missing something for years." Her frustration was vividly apparent as she told me how she felt about having been dismissed by the medical establishment for questioning a link between her various ailments and how she now feared she had let herself down.

She quickly moved on to the subject of her disillusionment with life in general. "I have the most amazing life," she said, throwing her arms in the air and then slamming both hands simultaneously on the leather arms below— before declaring, "But I've realized I'm not happy, and I don't know why. Is this why I'm sick?"

Ursula is a great example of someone who has managed to tick all the right boxes when it comes to achievements and lifestyle—not just personally, but also to meet the approval of her peers. I am sure she thought she was doing really well until she was brought up short by the health scare that threw everything she believed into free fall. Many people unconsciously and consciously exercise their "free will" in life and do everything they can to end up with a successful life on paper. The child in us prevails and the socially conditioned need to be a good boy or girl and do the right thing to survive still drives much of what we choose to do.

Perhaps Ursula deserves a pat on the back because she has worked hard and played hard and created an enviable life for herself. But has she created this life? Was this outcome (the glamorous life) her creation, driven by free will, or just a bit of luck, or maybe divine providence? These kinds of questions tend not to arise until we bump into something as serious as cancer and then try to work out what went wrong. Now faced with the possibility of a premature death, Ursula was convinced that she must have done something wrong to end up in this terrible situation—so what to do?

We certainly enjoy believing we have free will and have control of the events of our life. "You can do whatever you want"/"The world is your oyster!" This kind of rhetoric taps into a primitive part of us that habitually survives on many levels.

"Your father doesn't *want* anything," my mother used to scream as if "wanting" was next to Godliness and the absence of "wanting" a threat of annihilation. It's true that my father really didn't want anything other than some peace and quiet from her, which he only found behind the clatter of his electric mower or the din of commercial TV. Somehow over the past half century, "wanting things" has been dressed up as the new holy grail and not to show a proper sense of ambition is a crime.

For our purposes in this book, "free will" is the freedom to choose our point of perception and to choose where we put our attention. When our attention is rigidly lodged in our thinking mind—like following an outdated belief, or letting a physical symptom define our life—this constriction or attachment becomes a trap that will hinder us as we attempt to find the way Home.

> *"Destiny" is the limitless unfolding of the universe. It is the natural flow of your life as it emerges from "Home" and your "Self."*
>
> *How we choose to **perceive** this natural flow of life from the vantage point of our minds is called "free will."*

Take something as simple as you "reading this book." From your mind's perspective, the active choice of reading this page involves a personal decision that arises from free will. But step back and see it from "Home"—i.e. let "You" observe the mind and body in action—and so let destiny unfold. In a sense you have "split" and become

GERAD KITE

two "people." The first "person" (the mind) taking action, being observed by the second "person" (the Self).

At this early stage of the book this idea may be hard to grasp but I want to plant a seed now that will grow and develop as we proceed. You will gradually realize that there is a "You" at Home, watching a "you" which comprises your mind and its games and the events of your life as they unfold.

What "mind games" do you play? Take some time to be honest with yourself, as very often the games we play are so well crafted and have become such a part of our routine that we don't even know they're a game and assume it's the only way to live.

For example: you pose an "innocent" question to someone, like, "Have you seen the dog lead?" fully knowing that the other person has left it in the car. The other person realizes their error and is now on the back foot. "I think I left it in the car," they say sheepishly—and bingo, they're now at fault and you have taken the upper position.

This is no big deal, of course, but it's a way (often unconscious) that many of us seek to reestablish superiority when we might be feeling inferior and bad.

*Become aware of the "games" you play and, rather than judge them, **observe** them and see them for what they are. Once you see them from this more open perspective, you are in a much stronger position to decide whether to keep playing them, or to put them to bed. Making your way up the steps of the pendulum is a process of unburdening. If you recognize a "game" you no longer need, dump it here and now—it will help you move with greater ease as you take the next step on your way Home.*

STEP 3 | Behavior

"Oh, behave."
AUSTIN POWERS

Now, with the greater perspective of having reached the elevated height of Step 3, let's take a look at "behavior" and how this can distract you from coming Home.

In Step 1 you realized that we are all in thrall to the cult of "I," a collection of labels which can become deeply constricting and unhelpful; in Step 2 you saw how your mind can be the ruler of you rather than you of it, which is all the wrong way around. Now you'll step even further back to question not only your own behavior but also how you define or judge someone else by theirs.

Much like the way we observe a child's behavior we need to observe our own. "He's beautifully behaved," we say as the small child sits quietly and neatly at the dining table. "Good behavior" has become a virtue; but it is also a trap.

Could you imagine not worrying about the way you behave? Have you ever considered just doing what instinctively arises within you?

When I first see patients, my parting suggestion is that they "ride on the back" of our session together; meaning that they should try and act on what naturally arises within them, to turn off the judgmental head that thinks it knows it all.

You need to be aware of the difference between what your "gut" tells you vs. your mind, as they are often at odds with each other. The mind has taken the role of the judge who sits on the bench and surveys every natural movement of life and labels it as either right or wrong. Don't give it all your attention. It claims a faux authority over natural laws and creates (in part) what we call behavior—a mental construct that we believe to be permanent and fixed.

When I offered the idea of rejecting the mind's judgment as a possibility to someone recently they looked horrified. "But what if my gut told me to go out and kill people. Something has to stop me." We're so used to "authority" telling us what to do that we've lost the reflex and confidence to listen to our "gut." We're so habituated to gain wisdom and information from outside our selves we've completely forgotten that a life lived rooted "at Home" arises from Peace and Love and in this place we are never going to rise up and commit genocide. That kind of "behavior" can only emerge from an isolated and conflicted mind.

Knowing where our "behavior" comes from is important. We have, for example, cultural and socially learned behavior—how one should hold a knife is a simple but interesting example. I was told as a child there was a right way (forefinger on top of the knife) and I took this on board. When I got to school I saw my playmate hold his knife in a different way. He gripped it like a pen. Was he then wrong? Of course he was—my programming told me so, and he and I on some level were divided by this thought, which was reinforced when I asked my mother about it.

Is this not a madness? What we need to remember is that while social norms are part of life and many of these traditions, habits and behaviors serve us well, some-one somewhere made them up and passed them down. They're not real in the sense of something permanent or true. And you won't find your way "Home" in knowing how to behave at a dinner party.

Mentally, you are a composite of many influences—from your DNA to your parents' relationship, to your peers at school, messages in the media and your life ex-periences. As we grow and respond to the world around us we develop an idea of who we think we are and what we believe to be true. This construct gives us a personal viewpoint and a framework from which to live our lives, but if we are not open to reviewing these ideas and ac-tions they can equally become a trap and restrict our per-spective and movement.

It's a bit like being trapped in a space with one window. Every day you look out and see much the same thing and so you feel much the same way. Your mind, starved of new impulses, will tell you this is all there is, and so you eventually stop looking.

Over years of practice I've learned that most of what people tell you in a consultation isn't the full truth. It's not that they intentionally lie, but the past is a story that can be changed in the present and frequently is, as we all need to find reasons for things we don't understand.

Patients tell me that their relationship is in trouble because they put on weight, or their terrible backache is because they fell out of a tree 35 years ago, or that they can't sleep because their house is on a ley line, and even that they're angry because their grandfather lost his business in the 1920s. But, when people seek to line themselves up with their history, I can usually tell that there's something more going on.

We take things from our experiences and turn them into the "story" we tell about ourselves; we say we are impatient because our mother always made us wait for treats, or that we have a bad stomach because that's just how it is for all the men in our family. We think we're night owls because we can't sleep, or we have low blood sugar and that's why we need to binge occasionally. We reckon that we love the adrenaline of stress, or that we're just one of those people who gets sluggish and hiber-

GERAD KITE

nates in winter. I often ask patients how they feel right now, rather than collect past history, and if, as so often, the answer is "exhausted" or "depressed" or "stuck," my next question is to ask them why they don't change what they're doing and so try and change how they feel.

Recently I saw a new patient who had been trying to come off very addictive sleeping pills for five years. Some three years before she came to see me, doctors had discovered that she had acute ulcerative colitis, and after an operation to remove her colon she had been given the all-clear. I asked her what had been going on in her life in the years immediately before this diagnosis, and the first thing she burst out with was that her parents had an almost derelict house in Cornwall, and that they'd stuffed it with bric-a-brac from antiques shops. "They don't know how to look after themselves," she said, then, "I don't want to live like that."

She went on to say that in order to keep her parents' house under control, she'd been traveling from London to Cornwall every second weekend to check up on them. "Do your parents want your help?" I asked her.

"Oh no," she replied. "They like the mess."

"Why do you do it then? Isn't it a lot of hassle making the trip every two weeks?"

"I do it because I can't stand the mess," she insisted.

It gradually dawned on her that her weekend drives to Cornwall weren't about her parents after all, but about herself. She was trying to save them from the thing she most feared; that if she got sick again, there would be no one to look after her in her old age. She compensated for this with overbearing behavior toward her parents, who were apparently quite happy with their lives.

She worried, she said, all the time. She was sure her partner didn't really understand her, so how could he look after her in the future? But now, seeing her thoughts and behavior objectively, she realized that she could step back from this locked-in mental state and break the habit of displacing those concerns onto her parents. She also started to accept that her partner perhaps didn't have a perfect understanding of her—few people do—and to stop worrying about that and discover the peace and security that comes from being with her Self.

When people like this present themselves a certain way—in her case as the worrier and the carer—they have gone far beyond seeing their behavior and all the associated feelings as an imbalance or something inappropriate. They believe it as their only reality and scrap around for evidence to back it up.

CASE STUDY—JULIAN

Julian was an actor and son of a well-known artist. He'd been in therapy for years without making much progress, and had a diagnosis of depression. When he first walked into the treatment room, his eyes fixed and staring, it struck me that the atmosphere in the room was not one of depression—a dragging, sunken grayness—but instead of high tension and anxiety. He could only articulate this as "a black feeling."

Fear is often not given its due. People talk and write articles about depression and the devastating effect it can have, but how many people (and especially men with other men) can admit to feeling afraid, let alone take time off work for anxiety? It is not recognized as something that can be as chronic as an illness, and yet I see it cripple people over and again.

Julian said he could never settle. He worked most of the time at home writing screenplays and occasionally did some acting work in the West End. At home he would pace around the room, his mind darting about and coming up with thoughts too numerous to write down, and then he'd open a bottle of wine.

It seemed to me that both of these behaviors were a way of trying to burn out and then douse the fear. Only when he was too exhausted to do anything else could he finally sit down to work.

Julian responded particularly well to acupuncture treatment and of his own volition made a little pendulum with paper, cardboard and a butterfly clip to stick on his fridge so that he could monitor his moods. He also decided to only allow himself to open a bottle of wine if he could honestly say that he was in the "calm." And it worked—he didn't drink for a week, recognizing that he was emotionally all over the place. One week he went away and returned for his next appointment saying in surprise that he'd felt a difference; this time he'd settled in the calm and actually described his mood as "an absence of fear." Next time he came back, he had swung back into extreme anxiety but this time he recognized it for what it was—a feeling that would pass.

When Julian was a child his father would force him into his studio and sit him down at his side. The boy would be given paper and a pen and told to write stories as his father worked. They would sit together in silence for hours at a time, the little boy forcing himself not to fidget and fighting the urge to run about and play. It imbued him with a terrible feeling that as a seven-year-old he couldn't place, and this grew worse when his father would ask him to hand over the pieces of paper and let him read out what he'd written.

No one lives their life in a fixed state. You don't need to remain scared forever because of a childhood experience. Many of my patients describe aspects of their lives that sound absolutely miserable and yet they battle on as though they cannot possibly escape their situation. They have lost a sense of perspective.

They hate their job but feel unable to change it. They don't like where they live but they'll come out with a reel of reasons for staying there. Julian thought he had to drink to write and almost saddled himself with a serious alcohol problem in the process, without seeking to identify the source of the emotion that drove him to be so scared and restless.

IT'S AN UNCOMFORTABLE TRUTH that we humans create and carry around a lot of guilt, and other negative emotions that give rise to all kinds of troubling behavior.

In the absence of being at home in our Self, heartache seems to be part of our natural makeup, and even if there's nothing present in our day-to-day life to make us suffer, we will go out and find it. We're good at punishing ourselves and others, and many of us have well-crafted and sophisticated ways to create new burdens—hale and hearty parents who can't look after themselves, partners who will never understand us—which stops us being our selves and living our lives to the full from Home.

Step 3 is about throwing the rule book out of the window and seeing what's left. Do we still exist if we disregard all the rules? Has our rebellious action sent demonic shock waves through the bowels of the earth? Of course not. We're still the same person and more than likely our new behavior, rooted in the heart and speaking from

Truth, will serve us, and everyone around us, well. Even if we forget how to hold a knife, we'll still eat with care at a friend's lunch party—because we love them.

Giving yourself permission to "change your mind" is one of the greatest things you'll ever do for yourself.

Change your mind about everything that you feel needs to change. It takes practice, as we've been conditioned to create thoughts and hold on to them until they are like stones that we carry in sacks on our backs. We make arrangements in good faith, sometimes months in advance, crazily believing we'll know what's going on and how we'll feel in three months' time. But what if you don't feel like going out for an Indian meal when the appointed time arrives? Change your mind—it's good for you. Be kind and apologize and accept you may lose some of the friends that rigidly stick to every plan and cannot change their mind. That's okay too.

Go on—I urge you. Be a rebel. But don't rebel against what you see out there in the world. Rebel against your mind, your thoughts and your behavior.

Break the rules. If you normally turn left at the end of your street—turn right and take the longer route. Hide your phone for a day and don't check emails. See if the world falls apart.

Do anything where you challenge your own behavior. We must remember that so much of what we do is conditioned by our mind and that our mind will always seek to reinforce these patterns for its own survival and security. Confuse your mind—do something different.

This kind of activity will create cracks in your current form of thinking which is no bad thing. As Leonard Cohen said, "There's a crack in everything—that's how the light gets in."

"The most painful thing is losing yourself in the process of loving someone too much, and forgetting that you are special too."
ERNEST HEMINGWAY

In this step, you are going to examine your Self through your relationships with others. Often our attention is overly focused on the people around us. Step 4 reminds us of our primary Love—our Self.

Relationships are wonderful and inevitable but they can also be messy. Just as the weather will change outside your window, one moment calm, the next moment stormy, so will the dynamic between people. A relationship is possibly one of the best ways to rock the pendulum, but equally it can bring you back to the calm where you rediscover your Self.

A healthy balanced relationship is not necessarily dependent on a Waltons-esque environment. There are lots of different kinds of relationships—loving and warm, cold and tough; relationships where you are the leader, others where you are the follower; some based purely on sex. We need to be clear about what constitutes a healthy relationship and whether it serves us, or distracts us on our way Home.

The following testimonial from Catherine helps us appreciate how lost and confused we can become in a destructive relationship with someone else, and how this painful distraction can keep us from Home.

TESTIMONIAL—CATHERINE

When I first walked into Gerad's practice five years ago I had lost the sensation in my right arm and my fine motor skills were seriously affected. I had little energy and was in constant pain. I was 40 years old and the mother of two young children. We spoke in depth. Gerad was like a detective asking question after question. At that point, I was in a psychologically abusive marriage and, although well educated, had lost all my confidence and sense of self. I doubted my every thought and even questioned my sanity.

As our sessions continued, so did our penetrating discussions. Gradually, I came to see that I could not survive in my marriage. I was only just existing. My children deserved more and so did I.

As I gained physical strength, my mental strength improved. Or was it vice versa? Either way, I felt my power return, my sense of self, and I left my toxic relationship. I have never looked back, not for a millisecond. I came to the realization that my mentally disturbed husband had created this chaotic world and I had passively accepted his reality.

When I regained my strength, I knew I could no longer live in his world. I have been on my own now for two years. My energy has returned—my freedom. Occasionally, he does or says something damaging about, or toward, our children and I am thrown off kilter. But never for long, since I can recognize and speak the truth, and my children and I move forward again.

I have forgiven my ex-husband. I have let go of his abuse and cruelty. It lies in the past and I am living in the present now. He has no power over me anymore. I am free to live.

Catherine says she has forgiven her husband—but in truth she has forgiven herself for having allowed herself to live a life under the destructive shadow of cause and effect, far removed from the light and Love of Home.

Being in an unsatisfactory relationship (this is the only option for some people) is not a problem in itself as long as you admit it to yourself and see and accept it for what it is. For Catherine this was the key. And, in her case, when she awakened to the negative nature of her relationship and refound her strength, she had to take action.

Our relationships with others, no matter how casual and fleeting, or intimate and long-standing, act as a mirror to show us how we project ourselves into the world. A common mistake is to look at the people around us and to blame them for the challenging situations we find ourselves in.

"Perception is projection" is the philosophical theory that whatever we perceive externally is a direct projection of our self—our thinking mind. For example: if we don't like the way a person is treating us, they are only behaving that way because it's how we're choosing to interpret that behavior.

When I was training in Gestalt therapy, we were all obliged to take part in a "perception is projection" exercise. We took it in turns to sit on a chair in the middle of an empty room. Another chair was placed in front of us and one by one all classmates would come in and sit and proceed to tell us:

a. Their first impression.
b. How we made them feel.
c. Who they imagined we really were.

It was a fascinating process. Not only did we receive interesting feedback about ourselves, we also witnessed each person's projections onto us. The negative perception I had of myself at that time was transformed by the many appreciative comments I received, which were powerful enough to change my rather dark and diffident self-image.

When we are triggered emotionally we abandon the calm. We move away from Truth. We project our self-created thoughts and emotions onto each other and, just as a projectionist sets up his camera and projects a film, we force our fantasies onto each other and label them as truth. An authentic, loving relationship between two people can be trumped by the mind's projections which obscure Truth and block the way Home.

We react and bounce off each other all day long, rarely stopping to question our role in the creation of these situations. But our emotional triggers are close to the surface and if we have something brewing we can pretty quickly find someone who will act as a screen for what we want to project.

One of the most striking aspects of the partnership dynamic is the unspoken agreement that either one of the parties can safely "act out" (behave badly) and display all kinds of dysfunctional behavior but because it is within the safety of the relationship for the most part they get away with it. This seems to work until they wake up either to the truth of what they are doing, or the long-term damage of such a dynamic which ultimately traps them both.

TESTIMONIAL—JENNIFER

One month before our wedding day, Jay told me that his best friend Harvey had gone online and paid a dollar to be ordained as a minister so he could officiate our marriage. I was very upset by this news. It was further psychological evidence that Jay was resisting letting go of his best friend and our impending union. From the moment we got engaged I had felt Jay's and Harvey's bond grow closer in ways that excluded me. It was as if our marriage was a threat to their friendship which had begun when they were 14 years old. I spent a lot of time in pain, obsessively collecting evidence for my case against their friendship which I saw as a vehicle for Jay's avoidance of true intimacy with me.

One evening it all got really bad. Jay and Harvey went off together to participate in a group event led by a shaman—a spiritual journey was how Jay described it to me—and the participants' spouses and partners were not allowed to join the group. This was the straw that broke the camel's back. I felt that Jay had abandoned me at the most primal level. I alternately sobbed and stormed through the house, enraged by Jay's refusal to surrender to our marriage.

And then something happened.

It was an almost visual experience. The thick opaque

glass wall on which I had been projecting an image of "YOU DON'T LOVE ME" cracked. Standing behind that glass wall was the real Jay—the husband Jay who loved me then, had loved me all along, and had been doing his best to stay loving in the face of my anger and jealousy. I realized in that moment that I had been having a relationship with a projection of my own making. For the first time in our four-year-long relationship, I saw Jay.

Jennifer's story is not uncommon. Few people ever question that their perception of their relationship with another may not be true.

Have you ever examined your relationships in this way and put them under the microscope? Or do you prefer to keep them as they are and cherish the "story" of you? The more burdened you are by fantasies about your Self and your relationship with others the harder it will be to ascend the pendulum shaft and find your way Home.

Take some time to reflect on your relationships and ask your Self if your stories are true.

In our misguided search for peace, we can easily get confused when we think we've found Home in someone else. Our mind says, "There you go—you've found it," and we believe it and embrace this new person with all our heart.

The key insight here is to be clear if you are mistaken. If you are, you don't have to end the union; just be aware that many of the expectations not met in the relationship will never deliver as they're not the "Home" you're really looking for.

If you are still not sure—then remember this. The quality of Home is peaceful and permanent. The quality of relationships is chaotic and impermanent.

*"Realize deeply that the present moment is all you ever have.
Make the Now the primary focus of your life."*
ECKHART TOLLE

Being in the moment

Having completed Steps 1 to 4, your perspective has already changed. You can look up and away from the circumstantial ebb and flow of your life and begin to put your attention on what truly exists at the heart of You. Here. Now.

Climbing the steps of the pendulum is an act of faith. We talk about "my life" or "my problems" as if they are possessions that we carry around with us and which make us feel like somebody. But often, as we have seen, we give the events around us far too much credence and worse still create our identity around them. It is very difficult to be "in the moment" if we are carrying around a load of unresolved psychological baggage.

It's impossible to root yourself in the present when you're drunk with thoughts and emotions from the past or longing for something in the future.

The ancient Chinese philosophy of Taoism tells us our natural state (here and now) is one of contentment and Peace and is permanent and indestructible. This state lies at the core of everything and is the essence of humanity. Some people call this the "God within," but whatever name you want to give it, the important thing to remember is that it is not something you have to look for or create; it exists within the heart of all of us—right now. The challenge is to shift your attention to the Home inside and away from the layers of stories and illusions created by your mind.

I try to enlighten people on this when I see them worrying and fretting about different facets of their lives. They listen but look at me as if I am mad and then pile on more reasons for why they feel so bad. It's as if they're married to misery. That is not to say there are no real problems in our lives—there are; but they, like all things, come and go, just as in the natural world there are disasters that rise and fall. They are in the impermanent realm, whereas the peaceful root of Existence is permanent and silent and survives all surface noise. Remember this ancient wisdom: *"This too shall pass."*

If only

"If only we'd bought a house before the boom." "If only I'd started trying for a baby five years ago." "If only I was being trained in something more practical." "If only we could win some money." "If only I had heard about you earlier." "If only he would stop smoking."

In our culture playing the "if only" game, much like engaging in gossip, can feel compelling and attractive, but in truth it is something we do to avoid living in the present moment. "If only" takes us backward and forward, visiting stories of the past that has gone and the future that doesn't exist. It gives us a false "experience" which brings more pain and keeps us further from being true to our Self.

CASE STUDY—INDRA

Indra, the "Princess of Stories," was 33 when she first arrived at my clinic, with the story of her life so well formed in her mind and so convincingly delivered that I was briefly seduced into becoming a character in the story too. Her well-crafted tale told of the young Indra held hostage by repressive parents. Locked away from the temptations of the 1970s disco revolution, she wept most nights until one day a handsome young man named Paresh appeared at her door selling "spot the ball" coupons. This fateful night was the beginning of a great romance. After weeks of being wooed, she was climbing out of a window to scale the garage roof and setting up all sorts of clandestine meetings. These meetings went on for over a year until one night she waited by her window and Paresh did not come. She waited all night, too terrified to imagine what might have become of him, but he never came again.

This was the story Indra carried around almost like a favorite book tucked under her arm. Every time she came to see me she would find some way of taking us back there, adding new detail and color and reliving the pain. The true end of the story, which she omitted until one day I pressed her on it, was that she had fallen pregnant and told Paresh, hoping that he would be her Prince Charming and rescue her. In the end, she had had a termination in secret. Indra finally left home aged 28 and had been alone until she met her current partner two years later.

The amazing thing about Indra was that each time I heard her story, it had a freshness and vitality that made you feel it had all happened yesterday. She also had a story about the future: the house she and her husband would buy and the children they would have, all told with the same zest.

The one story she did not have was the one of her present. She seemed unable to relate anything to the here and now. Uninterested in her relationship and work, having few friends and no hobbies, she would do anything to avoid talking about who, what and where she was right now.

During treatment I encouraged her to start identifying how she was feeling right there in the room. I would ask her what she was doing today and would gently bring her back to the present every time she attempted to pull me into her stories. As our sessions together progressed, Indra began to look more closely at her life and told me how she had started to make changes in her routine, moving from full-time to a four-day week at work, inviting friends to her house and starting an exercise routine. It was fascinating to feel the change in her as the grip of her stories started to weaken. After three months she stopped mentioning them altogether.

Mind, Body *and* Spirit

"Mind, Body, Spirit" seems to pop up everywhere these days and has almost become a brand name for anything "alternative." But ask someone what these three words in combo actually mean and it's a struggle. That's because we no longer really know what "spirit" is. Everyone understands the "body" and "mind" of this trilogy, but they shy away from describing the third.

The difficulty with defining what the Spirit is, of

course, is that it lies beyond thoughts and words, and so paradoxically the key to understanding it mentally is accepting that you can't. It's a "feeling" thing. Think of the "goose bump" moment when the hairs on your neck and arms lift as something "touches" you beyond thought.

The ancient Chinese had little problem in recognizing and feeling the presence of Spirit in everyday life. It was essential. This was a culture which knew from bitter experience that to ignore it would be a threat to their own community and its long-term survival. They understood the "Oneness" and interconnectedness of all life, and how Spirit is the conduit between our inner and outer world. "As within—so without." This symbiotic relationship meant communication between the people and their environment was authentic and balanced and facilitated their success as a race.

In our sanitized modern world where our survival needs have changed, this natural connection has been greatly diminished. Instead, our minds have taken on the impossible task of providing us with an authentic sense of self and a meaningful direction in life.

Put simply—we are more than a body and a mind. The qualitative experience of being human comes from our Spirit and living from Home. We can listen to a piece of music with our physical ear, we can understand how it is composed with our mind, but the enjoyment and qualitative experience come from our Spirit.

Fake flowers can look impressive and beautiful; we can see them with our physical eye, and understand that they look real with our mind. Our Spirit, however, is not engaged.

Body communicates with body, mind with mind, and Spirit with Spirit. By shifting your attention back to the present, and being "at Home," allowing your body and mind to rest, you start the process of aligning your body and mind with your Spirit.

Being at Peace happens *now*. It is a moment that mirrors orgasm where everything appears to stop for an imperceptible moment, rendering us unable to think and only Be, as we are reminded of what it is like to be truly present.

One of the wonderful gifts of being human is that we can choose to shift our attention from one level of existence to another. We can shift our attention to our mind and resolve a puzzle, shift our attention to our body and dance, or shift back to "consciousness" and experience the Peace of thoughtlessness. When we change our focus, i.e. shift attention to the present moment, Peace and calm are the natural outcome.

The midpoint of the pendulum is the present moment, and any shift or movement out of this zone takes us into the past and the future.

Here, at the midpoint, we cannot be depressed by some gloomy reference to something in our past or some fear or anxiety about the future. Remember: the past and the future are there by virtue of memory and fantasy—courtesy of the mind—and neither are real in the "now."

Practically speaking, the best way to shift your attention away from your habitual, thinking mind is to wake up and "come to your senses." You are blessed with five senses that connect you to the outside world and form your inner reality and yet we only use a fraction of them, preferring to live from mind, or memory and fantasy.

As we prepare to move further up the pendulum and enter the World of Body, we need to reacquaint ourselves with the experience of being in physical form and this can only be done through our senses.

My training as an acupuncturist involved a profound rediscovery of my senses and a shift away from my "clever mind" and my pursuit of knowledge. To be an "instrument of nature" and serve my patients well I need to be able to "sense" them in every way and not make some kind of analytical diagnosis based on mental information and stories.

I invite you now to do the same. Get to know yourself through your senses. Smell everything, taste (and really taste) everything, see like your eyes are new, and hear the sounds around you like you just arrived from Mars—and become aware of all your emotions—without preference. In the "real" world of the senses, everything exists equally and this is the richness of life prior to the picky preferences of your judgmental mind.

Being in the moment, or coming to your senses, means exactly that—fully feeling and experiencing what is going on at the moment and starting the process of shifting your attention away from your mental state to the physical. This is what is explored in the next section—the World of Body. For example, if you shift your attention to your body—and you become aware of the chair beneath your legs, the smells in the room and the colors around you—you automatically stop thinking.

The way Home is a process of unburdening and waking up to what's here and now—as you begin to shift your focus to your own existence as an actual experience rather than a theory, and to avoid the distractions of the past and the future. Here at Step 5 I highly recommend that you engage in "true rest" by taking time out each day to do one of the things you've chosen to do to bring you back to the "calm." Get a meditation app and take 10 minutes, go and feed the birds or, if you haven't already, why not follow Graham's lead (our reformed "compulsive swinger") and make your own pendulum.

THE WORLD OF BODY

Surrender

"The human body is the best picture of the human soul."
LUDWIG WITTGENSTEIN

The World of Body contains just two steps which act like a bridge between the World of Mind and the World of Home. They are designed to help you understand and make contact with Natural Law and have a more profound relationship with your body.

These two steps have a more limited pendulum swing than the previous five steps due to their closer proximity to the pivot at the top.

In Step 6 we explore our physical form—the natural laws that govern us—and wake up to the fact that nature determines and guides our life. In Step 7 we look to the *cause* of our physical form—Love—and discover that this is the source of all "things."

The body is a child of Love and is the most loyal and generous friend you will ever have. It sits in a place of service and its only function is to give you the experience of being in human form. The body sits between our mind and our Self. It therefore has this unique position of being aligned with both. It receives instruction from Home and produces an outcome through thought. It is the sandwich filling that enables the whole experience of our life—fascinating and unique.

If we stop to think about how we come into being it is a miracle. The egg and sperm of our biological parents meet and become one. Our "Being" comes into existence. We exist. A few cells give rise to more and more until, not long after conception, our heart emerges from this bundle of cells and begins to direct our life. At this stage of our development we exist in form and this form has consciousness—not in the sense of being mentally conscious, but in the sense of our being alive. Consciousness is considered to be *"the state of being aware of and responsive to one's surroundings,"* but what does that really mean? A newborn baby is considered conscious because it is responding to external stimuli, but the baby has no awareness of being conscious—it is just responding and reacting to everything around him or her and that information is being recorded and that experience creates what we call the mind.

Let's just look briefly once again at this curious thing which is the mind. We talk about it all the time but what is it exactly? Is the mind a brain? The jelly-like organ beneath the skull? In the ancient Chinese tradition the brain and the mind were not linked. The "mind" was considered to be the sum total of the activities of all the organs that direct our outer life—for example, the liver having the capacity to store blood and make plans, the heart having the capacity to pump blood and produce love, the kidneys having the capacity to control water and to Know the depths of who we are.

The point here is that our physical body and its organs are far more important than we give them credit for. If it was true that your liver held the secret to making all your dreams come true—would you abuse it with excess alcohol and fatty foods? If it was true that your capacity to love your Self and others was down to the healthy function of your heart—would you not put all your attention there and listen to what it says? And what about the humble kidney which barely gets a look-in and is just seen as a filter that scrubs the blood? If you knew that the healthy functioning of this organ brought you a deep sense of peace and access to the truth of your own unique manifestation—would you not at least drink plenty of water and get to bed on time?

The more we shift our attention from what we see as our sophisticated mind to our physical form and the physical world around us, the closer we stand to the door of Home. It's one of the reasons we're drawn to the countryside, and why we enjoy being by a river or an ocean, or to spend time with children and animals. It's here that we're closer to our origin and the freedom of being our Self.

Most spiritual traditions teach the importance of a body-focused awareness and in particular the attention to the breath as a means to be fully present. Why is the breath the key to presence? The in-breath is our connection with the formless (heaven) and is pure, whereas the out-breath is our celebration of life and death, and the connection with form (earth), the breath having made contact with every cell of our physical being. When you seek to shift attention away from the mind, the practice of focusing on the breath will draw your attention back to your physical Being and beyond.

Our body is the physical realization of Grace and provides a space for the celebration of life. The quality of our human experience is dependent on the temple that is our body.

STEP 6 | Natural Law

*"To lose confidence in one's body is to lose
confidence in oneself."*
SIMONE DE BEAUVOIR

Up until this point we have looked only at what we already know about ourselves: that we identify as individuals (the "I"), with unique patterns of thought (those mind games) and behavior (the things we do)—and that from this place we form relationships with other people. Most importantly we recognize that we primarily live in our heads and rarely visit the NOW.

Here at Step 6, just past the midpoint of our journey and on the first step in the World of Body, you are going to slow down and spend some time exploring your self through your physical form. What may at first seem a more abstract and mystical world you'll come to realize is far more real than anything your mind could ever offer.

We now enter a world governed by "Natural Law," where our thinking blends and merges with the laws of nature. We will learn about our strengths and weaknesses through ancient wisdom—the Law of Five Elements and the Law of Midday/Midnight. And discover that in spite of thinking that our existence and the way we are are largely down to "us," in fact we only exist by the grace of nature's great plan and subject to her laws.

How we steer a steady course as we make our way Home to Peace is dependent on maintaining equilibrium. The pendulum, you will remember, taught us about the perils of getting lost in mental and emotional swings—in the push and pull of the thinking world. Now that we've stepped up and away from a mind-dominated reality we will begin to gain an awareness that a life lived from the World of Body governed by Natural Law is effortless— and that equilibrium is the natural process that will deliver us to the door of Home.

Let's start by looking at the philosophical backdrop to Natural Law. I want to emphasize here that there is no need for you to fully understand every aspect of what is described. At Step 6 our goal is *not* to gather more knowledge; but rather to retreat from our already overburdened minds—so I'll keep it as simple as possible.

A beginner's guide to Taoism

Five thousand years ago in ancient China, Taoist scholars and mystics developed a profound understanding of life based on a close study of nature. They studied nature not with a scientist's curiosity, but rather as a means of survival; since a failure to understand and work with her character and patterns could pose a serious threat.

This study was conducted through a sensory experience because the ancient Chinese understood that it is *only* through our senses that we stay connected with Truth and the natural flow of life. The same, of course, is true today, yet we've abandoned our intimate relationship with nature and loaded all our attention onto our minds.

The ancient Chinese knew about the miracle of being human and the interconnectedness of all life. They weren't concerned with the individual or the "I"; they understood that we are but small cogs in the machinery of the Universe as a whole.

But they were curious. How does this natural system evolve and maintain life? Through a profound and intimate experience of the natural world, they came to realize that the source of life (the Tao) is perfect, formless and eternal: and that this permanent state of perfection, by reflecting its own consummation is the creation of all form—including our world, and you and me.

The Tao is formless "space"—pure Awareness. And this ancient culture came to "Know" that everything exists by the grace of this limitless source of energy—be it a dog, a table or the moon. Just as we are now beginning to understand that the physical universe, the stars and the moons, emerge from "space"—so do we.

> *If you are struggling to conceive of this, perhaps take some time out to try and experience it, viscerally. Close your eyes—direct your attention to your five senses and become aware of how it feels to be in your body—right now.*
>
> *This tangible, sensory experience (however faint) is an echo of the Tao and Home—the Truth of who you are.*

The emergence (consummation) of life is explained in the principles of Yang and Yin—the first Natural Law—the law of opposites. Yang is the original act of life, the creative principle, and Yin is its opposite, the passive, destructive force and cause of death. The principles of Yin-Yang are present in every form; they are the building blocks of the Universe and, just like the working of a clock, Yin-Yang become tick-tock and time is born.

Natural Law states that all interactions and relationships between phenomena follow this natural order, and are based on this law of opposites. The ancient Chinese witnessed this in how the seasons followed an ordered and time-related pattern; e.g. spring emerging from winter and the growth of spring being destroyed in autumn.

They also observed that in spite of this natural and endless cycle, in certain years one season might fail and have consequences for the rest of the year. For example, if the winter was not cold enough to promote hibernation and rest, the growth in spring would be compromised, thereby reducing the yield in the harvest time of late summer.

They chose to name these different movements of life according to the tangible elements that predominated in each of the five distinct patterns they observed in the seasons (they split the summer into two parts: early and late). **Wood** was in abundance during the cycle of growth (spring), and **Fire**'s heat was peaking as it matured the crop (summer). **Earth** demonstrated its richness in the harvest (late summer), **Metal** and its heavy presence put pressure on the land to decompose (autumn) and **Water** being plentiful at this time offered regeneration (winter): five phases of one year.

*They named the pattern of the seasons, or phases, the Law of Five Elements. **And they saw that these patterns and movements operate within us in exactly the same way.** They create every aspect of who we are.*

However, when they saw that these patterns are mirrored in each one of us too, they certainly didn't mean that wood, for example, was growing inside us—rather that the qualities of wood derived from this very particular dynamic are essential for a human being, or any life form, to get up and "grow." Equally, the fire element is not an actual inner furnace but our capacity to produce warmth and be open and loving.

When we shift our attention to the Universal intelligence that exists within, we touch base with reality and connect with the rhythmic patterns of the Source (the Tao). By following Natural Law and working with nature you're another step closer to Home.

The Law of Five Elements

"My point is—life is about balance. The good and the bad. The highs and the lows. The pina and the colada."
ELLEN DEGENERES

The unique balance of the five elements that create and maintain you are the gift of your life. This is the foundation and reality of who you are. You are both a unique form and an integral part of Universal intelligence, flow and evolution.

When we feel well in ourselves and have an inner sense of peace, this is the direct outcome of the five elements maintaining balance, being in harmony with one another and "going with the flow"—the flow of life. The five elements give rise to every aspect of your being. Your internal organs, your internal systems, your body

GERAD KITE

parts, and the root of your thoughts and emotions—
all of this is the outcome of the five elements working
individually and collectively, governed by the natural
rhythms of life.

But just like nature as a whole, which can at times lose
balance, so do we.

In the following section we are going to look specifi-
cally at how how a lack of awareness or an imbalance can
cause us to lose our equilibrium, stray from the "calm,"
and even make us ill.

Wood—timidity to belligerence

We pretty much take it for granted that, when we wake
up in the morning and take the first step into our day,
these actions are of our own volition. But the truth is
that without the gift of the wood element this morning
ritual would not happen. It is a very normal daily activity
and is mirrored in all of nature and seen at its peak in the
season of spring, when nature has been asleep all winter
(or in our case, all night). The spring dawn is our natural
awakening. And, if well rested, as each new day dawns,
we easily reengage with our daily life.

The wood element gives us perspective, the capacity
to step back from the minutiae of our life and see the
bigger and wider picture. It's only through the resting
phase of winter (or nighttime) that the wood element can

review, assess, and make the corrections that will ensure survival for the following cycle.

When we fall asleep at night we're not just sleeping, we enter a profoundly busy process of inner growth and renewal, the results of which emerge the next day: a better and more efficient version of our self. It's a bit like downloading updates to your software on your computer—effortless and essential for the smooth running of your life.

The Chinese pictogram for "anger" is of a tree growing in a box; something that's not allowed to grow healthily in an unchecked fashion. When you have a primary imbalance in the wood element you struggle to get up and grow, and so you have a feeling of being restricted; either you have an abnormal amount of anger which may come shooting out of you at the vaguest provocation, or else you feel defeated, devoid of the assertiveness that could help you move and change. We tend to see anger as a negative emotion, and it can be when it is not used well, or flares up strongly, but it's also a driving force. Wood has the capacity to break through anything that stands in the way of truth. Wood is the general and the soldier rolled into one and has the job of directing and clearing the road so that life and evolution proceed as planned.

The way we move and position ourselves in life is no different from the way the trees and the plants of a forest "know" how to grow and make space for each other and ensure there is room for all their roots to reach down and for the leaves to reach up.

When the wood element begins to malfunction the natural traits of growth and renewal become confused and timing and coordination are disturbed. Rather than move through life with ease and grace, we meet obstacles head-on—or collapse before them. We get into conflict with people who do not share our views, bump into things we just don't see, and perceive the world as frustrating and "wrong." The power of wood, as evidenced in natural growth, is to be able to both advance *and* retreat, and when wood struggles, we either only want to push forward or can barely put one foot in front of the other.

Are you prone to being timid, choosing to say nothing while often feeling quietly cross? Or are you like a bull in a china shop—jumping in to argue your point of view and insist that you're right and "they" are all wrong?

CASE STUDY: WOOD

Alice and Chris had been together for almost ten years, but they made for uneasy company. His aggressive behavior and her passivity in the face of his attacks had become normal for both them and their immediate family and friends. But it came as a shock to anyone new in their lives.

Alice was unhappy and had been since she was diagnosed with postnatal depression after the birth of her daughter. The birth was traumatic and she conceived again very soon afterward and continued to feel depressed after the birth of their son.

Chris was her polar opposite—lively and entrepreneurial, he shot out of bed each day with a budding agenda for everyone and would impose it by barking instructions, repeating himself over and over again until his target broke and surrendered to his plan. When spring bursts forth from winter its need to be seen and heard is profound and enlivening but in Chris's case his release each day from the night before was crushing.

In the evening, with the kids safely in bed and Chris entertaining himself in the local pub, Alice would drink alone. She loved the feeling of the first glass of red wine with its soothing hit and the second with its soporific call to bed.

Apart from when she was semi-anesthetized from alcohol, Alice didn't know what it was like to be at peace. "This is how I am," she'd tell her mother when questioned. "I'm okay, I'm just a bit depressed—the doctor told me so."

When Alice came to me she said she wanted help with neck pain and headaches that she put down to carrying kids. I tried to find out more but her one-word answers were frustrating. I eventually gave up. Hiding was a skill of hers.

After about five sessions I decided to introduce "Two Chair work" in an attempt to coax Alice out from the extreme low she had got so used to living in. This style of therapy aims to help people by focusing on the person's primary emotional issue and confronting it with the opposite state.

The person is asked to move back and forth between two chairs, each representing one side of the issue. In this case, "Timid Alice" was put in one chair, and "Angry Alice" (the opposite) was introduced and put in the other. The idea was that by encouraging communication and union, balance would be achieved—and we'd get "Assertive Alice." Imagine "The Pendulum—Live."

I explained the process to Alice and the reason for doing the exercise and she reluctantly moved as directed into the "Timid Alice" chair and stared at her knees. "Timid Alice," I began. "Could you please tell Angry Alice how you are feeling." Once I had her attention I pointed to the "Angry Alice" chair. There was a long pause and then quite suddenly she barked at the empty chair in front of her, "You can fuck right off." Confused, I jumped in: "Alice, no . . . You have to move to the other chair to speak like that." At which point she stood up, picked up her bag and left the room.

I was taken aback, and concerned that I had totally misread both her and the situation. A month passed and an email appeared in my inbox—subject: "Sorry." She said that when I had told her to speak to "Angry Alice" in the opposite chair, all she could see was a mirror of the pathetic and tortured soul who had come that day for help, and she had been so shocked she had been unable to hold herself back. She had entered a prolonged state of fury, and described how she had gone into battle with anyone and everyone, exercising her anger wherever she could—and, to her surprise, she had loved it. She loved the energy that arose through conflict and the peace she would feel with each battle "won."

Then at last she had found herself settling back into the calm, and remembered her self—the woman she had left behind almost two decades earlier. She was now feeling filled with potential and able to enter a new cycle of growth.

Fire—joylessness to excitation

Feeling lighthearted, happy and loving are natural human traits. These feelings are rooted in the fire element and experienced as the "joy of Being."

We tend to misunderstand the real meaning of "joy." To "en-joy" something does not necessarily mean it is something we approve of, or have a preference for. To "en-joy" something means simply to be open to it and experience it from Love—no matter what it is. This sounds like a stretch, as why on earth would we experience "joy" in the face of something frightening or distressing? Well, because joy emerges from the compassion of Home, and compassion looks on all things *equally* and with Love. The beauty of the fire element is how it keeps our hearts open even in the face of danger.

The fire element is associated with summer, a time when we are closer to the sun and more aware of its power to open and warm our lives. The warmth of this element celebrates the gift of our humanity and blurs the boundaries created by our minds, beliefs and opinions as we merge with each other and remember that we are held together by friendship and Love. Situated at the top of the cycle, the fire element is closest to our source— our spiritual root—and helps us remember that we are all children of the universe, here to share and play.

The ancient Chinese saw the heart as the physical manifestation of fire. It was seen as an empty vessel with the capacity to receive and connect to the raw material of the cosmos that gives rise to all form. The heart is "Home" and the essence of freedom and maintains the correct relationship with Existence. It is the balancing point inside us that eventually brings us back to Peace.

When there is an imbalance in the fire element, we

take things too quickly to heart and experience insult deeply and painfully even when offense was not intended. In a reflex to protect ourselves, we pull back and close the gates around our heart. "You've hurt me—so I'll hurt you."

This lack of easy forgiveness can lead some into inappropriate friendships; there can be a desperate urge to be great mates straightaway—a need almost to engulf the other person. On the other hand it can take years for others to open up to someone and consider him or her to be a real and trusted friend. An imbalance in fire can mean the loss of that subtle skill to know where healthy boundaries lie.

Do you feel easily hurt by other people's thoughts and deeds? Are you kind and forgiving when your friends mess up or let you down, or are they cast into the wilderness never to be seen again?

CASE STUDY: FIRE

My patient Anna was a great teacher for me. She not only taught me about the fire element—but also about myself. At our first meeting her strong presence filled the small treatment room and the first thing she told me was that she wanted to be happy but needed to find a partner for that to happen. In the next breath she asked me if I was married. Her bold and intimidating style was seductive but it also felt aggressive and put me on my guard.

The nature of the rapport between the practitioner and patient is crucial to success in diagnosis and treatment. My own teacher told us many times to "love" our patients, as this meeting "in love" was key to rapport. The relationship is of course professional but it is also dependent on a certain openness and transparency which must be managed by the practitioner. The intimate dynamic needed to open the door to help someone discover their self is the domain of fire, but the volatility of this element can become a problem and is sometimes hard to contain.

Anna told me she had been depressed for years. She was 36, had a very successful career in public relations and was adored by a string of men who would do anything for her, but she said she hadn't found "the one." When she described these platonic relationships, she was effusive in her praise and reeled off the holidays and gifts they bought for her. It seemed strange to me that none of these "wonderful" men had made the grade, and that they persisted, surely knowing that they were never going to get what they wanted. Two of them had been "courting" her for over ten years.

As our sessions together continued I started to feel a disconcerting dynamic between Anna and me. It seemed I could never get it quite right with her, and I had to presume that whatever she was managing to induce in me was the same thing she brought about in all the other men in her life. I never knew how she would be: sometimes sweet and affectionate, at other times cold and shrill, making completely unreasonable demands. She tested every boundary I created, pushing me and seeing if she could cross it.

Each of the five elements has a "virtue" and for fire it's "propriety": the understanding of what is appropriate and acceptable in given situations. Fire, through its capacity to measure social and sexual temperature, gives us the "room" to move in and get close to someone and the subtle knowledge of when to retreat. Anna's social and emotional barometer was all over the place and she struggled with any kind of emotional intimacy.

She said she felt unloved and alone and yet she was so distrustful of her relationships that she was unable to accept love from anyone. She was a great example of someone with an imbalance in the fire element who possibly either didn't get the love she needed as a child or was given no boundaries, but more importantly she didn't know how to generate love for herself.

The problem was that Anna was convinced that the "love" she needed was to be found outside her Self. She couldn't be alone, she was always on the phone, always planning the next thing. Sadly, I never got to see if I could truly help her. Her life ended suddenly in her mid-40s after a short illness. Even in her final days, surrounded by people who cared for her, she couldn't make peace with the world, her determination to maintain control still blocking the flow and ease of love.

Earth—satisfaction to starvation

"Satisfaction" is a wonderful feeling and nature demonstrates this in the season of late summer—this is the harvest season when the earth element gives us the capacity to count our blessings, and store that experience within ourselves for when times get tough.

It is the earth element that provides us with the capacity to look out into the world and "think" about what we need and how to get it. Nature teaches us that the produce of the harvest needs to be securely stashed away so that in the depths of winter we can go into the storehouse, and find the bare essentials to survive. For many of us, of course, the practical ritual of preparing for winter is no longer a pressing need as we can go shopping 24/7 with a few clicks on the Web, and simply flick on the heating. But unless we truly take in and nurture a sense of inner security by savoring our life experiences and the joy of our friendships, in fact, everything that gives us a sense of our self and our place in the world, we can begin to feel depleted and anxious—even when all our emotional and material needs in real time have already been met.

This element gives us the power to take anything and transform it into our self. For example: we take it for granted that, when we eat a meal, this action settles our hunger and gives us energy. The truth is that by eating a meal we take that fuel into our being and transform it into "us." It allows us to enjoy the wonderful experience of being connected in the most substantial way with the wider natural world. When we smell a beautiful flower, that scent is drawn in and turned into an experience that is stored inside. Everything that we absorb and layer inside ourselves is by the grace of the earth element.

We all have good and bad times. There are moments in life when we need others for us to survive and times when we are that rock for them. The earth element governs reciprocity, the importance of sharing and caring, giving and receiving.

When the earth element begins to fail, the natural motion of "give and take" in us becomes labored and loses its rhythm. Our instinctual understanding of what we need and what to avoid is confused. While barely able to meet our own needs, we may spend hours working on something for someone else—often something they don't even need. We can easily get fixated on all that we don't have rather than the wealth of what we do have.

Do you ever feel like there's just never enough—no

matter what you do? That you are always the one to encourage and congratulate others while they don't seem to do the same for you? Or are you able to "reap your harvest" and know you're okay?

CASE STUDY: EARTH

Daniel was a successful singer and his audiences loved him. But most of the time when he wasn't singing he was worrying. He worried so much sometimes he didn't even realize he was doing it. Instead he soothed the churning feelings in his stomach by filing every detail of his life in storage boxes. Bus tickets, letters, sweet wrappers, the odd menu from a fancy restaurant—almost everything you could imagine was filed away. He loved to go to his box files and visit the past.

Unsurprisingly, Daniel found it difficult to enter into long-term intimate relationships, mainly because the presence of someone else and all their stuff (physical and emotional) was too overwhelming and distracting. His answer to this confusion was to obsess over someone from a distance, and in some cases actually pursue them in secret.

Daniel came to me severely depressed, aware that each new "hit" he pursued was giving him diminishing returns. His friends had seen that something was wrong and offered their help. But being exposed in this way made him furious.

The reciprocal nature of mutual care is something we learn in early life and it is the earth element that manages and balances this seemingly instinctive act. When we are infants, our parents wean us and the "mother earth" within is activated. We learn to receive the good things of life and take them in, and then we learn how to share, and from then on the earth element assumes the role of parenting ("mothering") us and ensures we get what we need to survive while simultaneously understanding the needs of others.

Daniel choked on the care on offer. Unable to work, he continued to collapse in on himself, losing weight, and losing friends.

And then, one morning in late September (the harvest season of the earth element), the sun's different angle seemed to trigger something latent deep inside him and recharge life with its truths. Quite spontaneously he got up and began to sing. His frail body took over from his confused mind and he sang. It was like a call from grace—in this moment he knew that this gift of being a singer was still intact within him, this was his harvest, his reward for having dedicated years to perfecting his art, but also a lesson in humility as he realized that being a gifted singer was not his to own or destroy.

The ancient Chinese teach us that the virtue of the earth element is "integrity." In this context it is the earth element that provides the wholeness and stability that hold the center of life. Earth integrates everything, and to be truly well we need to integrate every aspect of what it is to be human. We need to "carry water and chop wood," in other words we must not neglect our humble role of worker by getting lost in our minds or becoming spiritually lofty.

Metal—disconnection to inspiration

The metal element is associated with the season of autumn, profoundly beautiful but also crushing, for the fall is when we are compelled to let go of the warmth of summer and begin the descent into darker nights, colder temperatures, knowing that the bleak midwinter is around the corner.

Metal has the power to take everything and condense it all into the purest of forms. It can only do this through a process of destruction, ruthlessly discarding anything that is extraneous. Our attachment to the external and frothy exuberance of life is now shifted to a more precious and profound focus—the ultimate goal of purity and perfection. The metal element gives the whole cycle of life its true value.

In autumn we feel an urgency; a sense of change and preparation. One day a tree is poignantly beautiful with its autumnal colors glistening like a jewel box, the next a dying structure devoid of color and life. This is a stark reminder that everything is temporary, and that the law of opposites is always in force. Metal teaches us the importance of letting go of all our attachments. Just as a hot air balloon will lift to the skies as bags of sand are dropped to the ground, so too do we feel cleansed and uplifted within ourselves as old habits, outdated ideas and unnecessary material goods are left behind.

Above all, metal gives us an inner sense of value that cannot be derived from external pursuits and acquisitions. Often, when we struggle to feel of worth, in a desperate attempt to distract ourselves we spread glitter on the surface.

There is a term used in the bible to describe a hypocrite—the "whited sepulchre"—the sepulchre being a small place for the dead and "whited" something that has become purified or bleached white. This image shows what happens to us when we have "died" inside and yet on the surface are still trying to put a gloss on things.

The metal element helps us understand the impermanence of our outer life. It is the means by which we stay connected to heaven—our nonmaterial Source, the breath that maintains our human existence from beginning to end. When metal is strong it roots us in the quality of the present moment but when it is weakened we go searching in our past and future for a sense of value. It becomes really hard to connect with the here and now. When we're locked in this state we get lost in regret and resentment.

Take a minute to work out if you value yourself. Do you look inside and like what you see? Or do you fear the void within? A profound mistrust of the quality of what we feel inside can produce a dark and lonely world giving rise to behavior that is a self-fulfilling prophecy of disappointment and loss.

CASE STUDY: METAL

Belinda was just 18 when without much warning her family collapsed around her ears. Her mother, in her 50s, had developed an eating disorder; her suddenly absent father had gone bankrupt, and was defined as a "crook" by her mother; and her 16-year-old brother had just come out as gay. In three short months the life she thought was perfect and permanent resembled a script from a soap opera and she was thrown into depression.

Her way of handling the events was to harm herself.

"Why are you cutting yourself?" I asked as I took her arm to find an acupuncture point. "I don't know really," she retorted. "For fun?"

Belinda's young life (by her standards) had been destroyed. Her sense of identity and self-worth was bound up in the privileged story of her childhood. She went to school with celebrities' kids, ate sushi at lunchtime and went skiing in the holidays and now here she was discovering that none of it was "true."

Most troubling to me was her disappointment over her father (our archetypal God within), a man who had collapsed mentally and physically under the stress of a failed business and the loss of his family. "I hope he rots in hell," she told me.

A few weeks into treatment Belinda started to let me into her dark world, announcing that she had a "secret." She told me that her father had made sexual advances toward her when she was younger and that she was going to go to the police to report him. Naturally I was shocked by this confession and at the time I had no problem in believing what she told me. And yet the way that this information was delivered also made me wary; a devastating time in her life was about to be used as a weapon when it needed to be carefully handled.

It soon emerged that, for all of Belinda's judgments of her family, and others, there was no one she deemed as terrible as herself. She told me she had always hated herself—never feeling attractive—and that she thought she was stupid. Her starting point had always been one of perfection; anything short of that was unacceptable and for as long as the family projected their ideal image out into the world, her superficial (and exhausting) confidence was sustained.

Many of us face massive disruptions in our young lives and we feel disappointed with how things change or turn out but, for someone with a primary imbalance in metal, like Belinda, such a chain of events validates an already existent inner dialogue of negativity and loss. When metal is weak our inner value system crumbles and all our perceptions arise from this place.

Over the following weeks Belinda talked and talked until there was nothing left to say. She ripped everyone and everything apart. It turned out her "flawed" father had been having an affair: she had invented her story of his sexual advances to punish him.

She started to get some clarity as she embraced her own imperfect world. Armed with an understanding of the need to find the treasure within and to trust that it was there, Belinda slowly but steadily discovered the uniqueness of herself—the metal that validated her life.

Water—fearlessness to terror

The water element is the base element and is associated with winter—the season of death, regeneration and survival. In this phase, everything in nature is still and quiet. Energy and power are hidden and low.

From an elemental point of view, this is the closest we can get to Home. The water element was considered by the ancient Chinese to be the origin of all life and the first element in the order of how the five elements brought everything into manifestation. The water element and winter both demonstrate the simplicity of Being. When we look across a winter landscape, we see an empty space, trees like skeletons hunched and frozen in the cold, the sun low in the sky casting long shadows across a barren land. In the absence of external stimulus we have little choice other than to retreat inside, away from our thoughts and back to a more contemplative place.

For some of us the introspective call of water is frightening. So much of our identity is bound up in the activity and materiality of our existence, we're not in the habit of asking, "Who am I?" If we lost our memory, our possessions, our clothes and found ourselves lying exposed and alone in that winter landscape—who would we be? Water holds the answer to that question. It has the capacity to store our essential nature prior to any of the activity and forms that we collect along the way and call our selves.

When we surrender to this element we discover that we find something primitive and true—as true as our DNA and the cause of who we are.

We all need fear to survive. Fear alerts us to danger and gives us the energy for "fight-or-flight." But when we have an imbalance in water, this automatic reflex is often lacking. We become takers of huge risks. Equally, we can swing the other way and become abnormally afraid of everyday life. We can develop all kinds of phobias as our underlying anxiety is projected out onto different situations.

Do you have a deep sense of yourself? If all your labels of who you think you are were taken away—would you know who you are? Are you afraid of death and not existing anymore? Or do you not care and move through life fearlessly, happy to try new experiences, new things?

CASE STUDY: WATER

Michael was a "still waters run deep" kinda guy— engaging and friendly, but also at times challenging and downright scary. His gregarious nature masked a depth of emotion that I don't think even he knew was there.

When Michael was a young teenager his father had disappeared from the family home, at first being registered as missing and later discovered living with a new woman on the other side of town. This was obviously shocking for anyone, yet Michael appeared on the surface to take it in his stride. It was around this time that he discovered judo, a discipline that is all about finding and cultivating the power within. Michael moved quickly up the ranks adding belt after belt and eventually reached one of the highest levels attainable.

The power of water is by its nature concealed. In his private life Michael maintained a relatively conservative veneer, living with his girlfriend, studying at university. He was highly accomplished at the midpoint of the pendulum, having spent most of his childhood upstairs in his room alone, but something within him was building in force and it wouldn't be long before this would need some further expression.

The first evidence of this was his decision to go to Australia and train as a stuntman. He was soon jumping off the top of buildings at a theme park in China. But Michael was still Michael and at home he'd turn off an electric wall socket with an eraser on the top of a pencil (just in case the switch was live). This was his world. The bubbling adrenal reality that lived within him had to be managed on a daily basis. It was exhausting for him.

When his relationship with his girlfriend came to an

end, he moved to London and burst out of his shell. Blissfully ignorant of the effect he had on people, Michael bounced from situation to situation, rarely attaching anywhere and always returning to the peace of his room.

Michael was self-reliant. His ability to disengage from his mind was at times perceived by others as a sign of distance or even naïveté, but for him it was part of a firm commitment to an honesty of being that many people spend years trying to achieve as they try to untangle themselves from acquired knowledge and beliefs.

I once spent a long time talking with him about an issue that I thought was important. All of a sudden, he seemed just to shut down. We were in a busy restaurant and it was hard to hear each other. "What are you thinking?" I asked him. "I'm just counting the bricks," he replied, and pointed to the exposed brick wall next to us.

Michael eventually discovered his perfect career, Five-Element acupuncture. He was able to draw on a discipline cultivated during his years of practicing judo, the confidence he found through acting, and most importantly his natural gift for seeking out the truth and getting to the point in hand.

These traits can all be seen in the water element.

Elemental triggers

As we have seen, the five elements work together as a team, adjusting for each new situation that life presents. For example, if someone or something frustrates you, the wood element asserts itself and gives you the capacity to step back, assess the situation and take the appropriate action; or, if you are in danger, the water element responds by producing the emotion fear, secretes adrenaline into your bloodstream and gives you the power to run for your life. When you respond spontaneously and appropriately, you can comfortably roll with the flux of life. However, when any one of the elements goes out of balance, and fails to provide its integral contribution to the whole, there is automatically a level of disharmony among *all* the other elements, which, having been alerted to danger, unify and react and send out a specific distress call relating to the cause.

Each of the elements manifests and has a corresponding odor, color, sound and emotion, and when a particular element is out of balance there are signs which we, as five-element practitioners, learn to read—changes in the sound of a person's voice, the color in their face, the odor coming from their body and their overall emotional tone.

But in fact we are all of us naturally endowed with the ability to read each other's body language, voice and mood; we do it all the time. We react to smells in the street even if only unconsciously, crossing the road without thinking, or suddenly feeling hungry because of a whiff of fresh bread from a bakery. We know when someone in front of us in a queue is agitated or threatening. Think of the way that a mother can catch the tone in her child's voice before more than a dozen words are said on the phone and know instantly that he or she is sad, excited, angry or in need. Parents watch their children and lovers watch their partners the whole time. If we pick up the slightest change in how they are, or in how they move and smell, we react. It doesn't matter what they say, because we have already sensed the direction their feelings have taken. The problem is that we are often better at reading other people's emotional states than our own. How do we know when one of the elements has failed in ourselves?

Our elemental triggers are simply another way of describing the cause of our emotional (pendulum) swings; they have the capacity to draw our attention away from the absolute Peace of Being—and down to the *relative* peace and chaos of our mind, and the extremes of our emotions.

Once you are aware of how you can be "triggered"—that is, which elements in you are the cause of imbalance—this awareness alone can shift your attention back to the calm.

If you believe mood swings are your only option ("That's just the way I am"), any attempt to climb the pendulum will be hampered and your reality will remain in the world of the mind and its drama.

For example: I'm sitting happily writing away and an email pops into my inbox. It's from the husband of a patient who is clearly upset with me. He accuses me of neglecting his wife because of my lack of availability at a time when she is unwell. This suggestion that I am not caring for my patients is a massive trigger for me (a weakness in the fire element). I take the accusation personally. How can he say that? I feel I am being unfairly attacked. What can I do? I now have two options.

1. Ride the pendulum swing. Feel and use the insult and hurt at the low, to gather strength for a counterattack in the high—which will end with me banging out a defensive email that I will very likely come to regret.

2. Observe the internal swing, feel the insult and the anger and the need for revenge but shift my point of perception to the Absolute Calm and watch the drama pass me by.

Most of us take option 1. It's easy to justify such a reaction—we're masters at it. We've taken our elemental triggers and turned them into virtues that we think protect the person we are—but they ultimately backfire and disturb the peace. The beauty of looking at ourselves through the prism of the Law of Five Elements is that it can release us from long-ingrained character traits that we have come to see as fixed and irrevocable.

The five elements teach us that none of us is quite so substantial as we think. We are all, in the end, just a collection of movements. If you have had a bad year at work, or a relationship has gone wrong for seemingly the same reasons as your previous one did, the important thing is not to let this become your life's work, but to recognize it as merely part of the impermanent nature of who you are, who we all are, our natures constantly in a state of flux as the underlying balance of the five elements in us is disturbed and compromised by external influences.

Once we reach the top of the pendulum, the loving and forgiving place of Home, we realize that there's room for everything. We see that we do not have to react or actively change anything. There's no need for any judgment—in fact it gets in the way. Everything has a right to exist equally and *self*-awareness is the only thing that matters in this process. It is only through the dismantling of who we "think" we are that we can get clarity—remember, it is the illusory self (our thinking mind) which keeps us handcuffed, and its habits and ways of being that restrict the natural movement of life.

The journey Home is a process of waking up to the full

reality of who you are. If you spend your whole life living through your thoughts, your memories and fantasies—it really is like living in a dream. As I said at the beginning of this chapter—it is only when we start to live through our senses, as we did as babies and young children, that we return to the natural world.

In this section, you will have begun to recognize many of the personal traits that you will (until now) have put down to your "personality." As you become familiar with how each of the five elements operates in you, and the triggers that trip you up and distract you from peace, you will start to see that the things you love and loathe in yourself and others are merely the dynamic dance of the five elements moving in and out of balance. Once you have this awareness, this shift in your point of perception, you will naturally relax and start to live in the present moment, accepting the variety of your life *without* judgment, avoiding the dramas and developing compassion for everyone and everything.

The Law of Midday/Midnight

The overall goal of Step 6 is to leave the World of Mind behind and to enter the slipstream of life's natural flow. Our starting point has been to understand the Law of

Five Elements and to develop an awareness of how "elemental triggers" can keep us attached to our thinking minds.

Now we move on and inward and discover how the organs and functions of our body are contained within the elements. At a deep level, these organs and functions are "portals" or "receivers" that have a direct connection and relationship with the universal flow of life (the Tao), and ensure that we stay synchronized with it.

Here I will teach you about the second law I mentioned—the Law of Midday/Midnight. This is a practical guide in how to reenter and stay within this flow. I will show you how to "reset" your system using ancient wisdom—the Chinese Clock.

MOST SELF-HELP BOOKS that focus on physical health come with a long list of do's and don'ts. They tell us what to eat, how to exercise, and a slew of other prescriptive directions. For some people, creating the right conditions to be fit and well has become almost a full-time job, or certainly takes up a huge amount of their waking day. So much so that this has become an imposition of the mind, rather than the body dictating its needs. It's a bit like the employees of a company telling their boss how to run the business in spite of not really knowing what's going on in it.

Our mind does not understand the complexities and uniqueness of the workings of our body. It is only the body that knows what it needs and when it needs it.

Many of the people I have helped over the past three decades have come to me because they want to be fit, happy and well. But they don't always connect this desire with taking care of themselves physically. Some will have done very little to listen to their body or look after themselves; while others will have read everything on the subject and have put together a health regimen that is more like a military operation than an act of love and respect.

For example—Sally thinks she knows what she wants and that she knows how to get it. She wants the body of a supermodel, a high-powered career and she also wants to get pregnant—oh, and to run the marathon, so morning begins at 6 a.m. with a pint of water, a 30-minute run, 20 vitamin pills and seaweed on wholemeal toast. Then she's off to a yoga class with just enough time to get to work at 9 a.m. It's day 14 of her cycle and the ovulation test says "yes" so she makes a quick phone call to John to check he will be home by 7 p.m. (she read somewhere this is the best time for sex as her cervical mucus will be at its most copious . . .). For John, this new life of abstinence, enforced relaxation, fitness training every morning at 6:30 a.m., and timed sex is taking its toll and he doesn't feel good. But they press on . . .

Our body knows what it needs, its gifts and limitations, and it will tell us if we listen. Sometimes when I'm working with people I ask them to do something specific like eating a decent breakfast or getting a certain amount of exercise, as without the basics in place the distraction of hunger or inertia will get in the way. But it's by no means a militant approach. The most interesting thing is to see the choices people begin to make when they step back from their calculating minds and all the information they've collected and start listening to their own unique wisdom inside. Maybe they'd rather parasail once a week than go to the gym every day, or eat oysters because they enjoy them and it makes them happier than a zinc supplement. Or go out for a big night with the lads—because it's fun. Health doesn't always have to be "healthy."

The Law of Midday/Midnight helps us develop an awareness of how the natural movements of life organize our physical form and offer us the opportunity to step back from our conscious mind and experience living through our instinctive, visceral Self. Without realizing it, many people are maintaining a routine that seems healthy, but isn't remotely natural or good for them.

Violating Natural Law

All of us violate natural laws every day of our lives. We ignore hunger when our stomach rumbles, eat when we're thirsty, take a painkiller for a headache when we know we should stop and rest, and avoid confrontation when actually that might be the best way of moving on in our life.

Some people are born with innate resources and strong constitutions. This means they can get away with pushing against the natural laws. Others have a weak constitution or live in difficult circumstances, and they constantly have to bring themselves back to that center of premium function, bolstering themselves with extra sleep, good food choices, and being more careful with their energy. You need to have a sense of your own limitations as an individual and not expect yourself to be able to cope with the same level of activities as others around you. You may be able to get by with less sleep than them, or you may need more. When you are in touch with your body and needs, you will be better able to judge this.

As we get older, we often accept low-grade health as a norm. We feel "tired all the time" but don't connect it to not eating properly or exercising enough, or taking breaks from staring at a screen. We get used to being stressed and anxious as the little vices accumulate. The story of the frog in the pot of water is a great analogy of our failure to recognize how we have gone out of balance.

"If you drop a frog in a pot of boiling water, it will of course frantically try to clamber out. But if you place it gently in

*a pot of tepid water and turn the heat on low, it will float
there quite placidly. As the water gradually heats up, the frog
will sink into a tranquil stupor, exactly like one of us in a
hot bath, and before long, with a smile on its face, it will
unresistingly allow itself to be boiled to death . . ."*

VERSION OF THE STORY FROM DANIEL QUINN'S

THE STORY OF B

You wake up tired, so you kick-start yourself with
caffeine before heading to a stressful work environment
that causes your cortisol levels to soar. You shovel down
a sandwich at your desk and barely taste it. More coffee
or tea to stave off that dip in the afternoon, and then by
the time work is over you're cross-eyed and edgy, so of
course you have an alcoholic drink to take the edge off.

It's not that we're incapable of feeling as energized
and relaxed in our late 30s and early 40s as we were in
our 20s, it's just that we lose the ability to see that we
are moving further and further out of balance and away
from Home. Our body has been designed with a perfect
clock, so from the outset "good habits" are latent in us.
The trouble is that our habit of defaulting to our heads
usually ends up with us overruling our inner clock. We
think we can stay up all night and then keep up our usual
routine the following week without any difficulty, and
are surprised when we find we can't.

I have one client who works as a stage manager in a

large, busy theater which means that he only works during the evening. This wouldn't be a problem in itself if he stabilized the rest of his time, but he wakes at 11 a.m. or 12 p.m., when he insists that he's not hungry, so keeps topped up on juice and hot drinks until 5 p.m., when he goes to the theater for the evening. The atmosphere backstage is frenetic and he's at the center of it all, instructing stagehands and making sure that actors and props are waiting at the right entrances. He still hasn't eaten anything by the time he gets home at midnight, when he makes himself comfortable with a book, music he loves and a big take-away dinner. He sits up till about 2 a.m., trying to wind down, and then he goes to bed with a full stomach and sleeps badly, only to begin the cycle all over again. I've suggested that he maybe eats a proper breakfast when he gets up, meets a friend for lunch and has a light snack after the theater and before bed, but he insists that it would be cruel to deprive himself of this sacrosanct comfort zone. He's had the same habit for more than 20 years now, and has persuaded his body that it's not hungry for 22 of 24 hours of the day, setting in train an odd cycle of deprivation and indulgence.

There is a point where nature will not allow us to continue pushing ourselves in this way. This point manifests in the form of physical or emotional symptoms or even a spiritual crisis that tells us we have to stop and look at what is going on in our life and with our health. We need to understand that these symptoms are offering us an opportunity to step back and change something.

When we live in synch with our external world, listen to our bodies and have the humility to admit that our clever minds with all their researched information might have got it wrong—when nature is given the chance to do what it is designed to do and we surrender ourselves to its plan—almost anything is possible.

The Chinese Clock

Nature has designed us in such a way that every part of us will function at its best when we are in synch with our environment. The Law of Midday/Midnight is a body "clock," which runs for a 24-hour cycle and reflects the changing rhythms of day and night.

As you can see from the diagram on the next page, the 24-hour cycle is made up of 12 x two-hour periods. In each of these two-hour periods, one of your ten organs and two "functions" (more on these shortly) that reside within one of the five elements is in the ascendant, and benefits from an increased supply of energy—the peak flow. First it's the lungs, next the bowel, then the stomach, then the spleen, etc., each organ enjoying a two-hour high point, a window of opportunity to function at their optimum. Conversely, the organs or functions at the

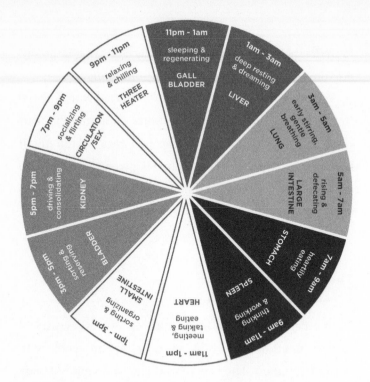

opposite side of the clock have less energy, and experience their low point—a time to rest.

I explained earlier how imbalances in the five elements are frequently dismissed as personality traits; so too can disturbances in the Chinese Clock give rise to problematic symptoms and inappropriate behavior. For example many people say that they are not "morning people" and accept that half of the working day is written off. Others slump midafternoon calling it a "carb crash," and some who are stuck to the sofa believe that an evening in front of the TV is all they can manage. All these symptoms tell us our "clock" is running out of synch and our connection to Home is being lost.

The Law of Midday/Midnight teaches us the importance of rest and play and to respect the enormous and complex tasks the organs do for us daily to ensure our health, and our survival. By ignoring this law we put extra pressure on these organs (the "Officials") and our system as a whole. The importance of the team effort is again emphasized here as any disturbance in any one period of the clock will immediately have a knock-on effect through the rest of the 24-hour cycle. When you work with nature's time schedule, all areas of your health improve and your whole system runs in one rhythm like a well-oiled machine.

As I say, the clock works on a cycle and it operates similarly to the tides of the ocean. The volume of energy in our body also rises and falls like water and the tides, but in this environment it moves in the shape of a figure of eight around our body, bringing highs and lows, according to how our organs and functions work and rest internally.

3 a.m.–7 a.m. (Metal)

We can start our journey at any point, but the early stirrings of a new day are a good place to begin. The hours between 3 a.m. and 7 a.m. are the "high tide" when the

lungs (3 a.m.–5 a.m.) and **colon** (5 a.m.–7 a.m.) are prioritized. For the first two hours your lungs benefit from the cycle's surge of increased energy, enlarging their capacity, awakening and oxygenating every cell in your body and every corner of your mind as evidenced by our active dream state at this time.

From 5 a.m. to 7 a.m., the peak flow shifts to the colon, making the morning the optimal time to rise, have a bowel movement and release the physical and mental waste of the previous day. You'll remember the metal element is responsible for maintaining the "quality" of your health, and this is the period when metal is to the fore, directing the taking in of fresh air and the release of all waste.

The metal element and our first breath are a gift of "heaven" and set the natural agenda of life that teaches us that nature gives before it takes. Life is bookended by the metal element. When the lungs open and expand to receive the fresh morning air, just as an in-breath results in an out-breath, the colon contracts (or "exhales"). Nature ordains that all waste be removed at this time, and so in good health we empty our bowels, and shower away the waste from our outer lung—our skin.

7 a.m.–11 a.m. (Earth)

Not surprisingly, the **stomach** is king over the next two hours, as the energy moves out of the colon and surges into the earth element, stimulating hunger and providing the energy to digest almost anything. The old saying that you should breakfast like a king and dine like a pauper is apposite. It's very basic—"nature abhors a vacuum"—and as you empty the lower part of your digestive system you refill from the top. You need enough fuel for the day. Would you really set off on a long car journey with no fuel in the tank?

The next stage from 9 a.m. to 11 a.m. is when the **spleen** is handed the energy baton and swings into action—transforming your intake into something usable for both physical and mental consumption and transporting it to every part of you, to provide the resources to move every muscle and get good thinking and working done.

11 a.m.–3 p.m. (Fire)

The **heart** receives its peak charge and rules from 11 a.m. to 1 p.m., at the height of the day when nature dictates that this is the time to back off from the business and activities of the morning, take a break—relax and socialize. The **small intestine** then steps in and gets to work to filter and organize from 1 p.m. to 3 p.m., sorting and clearing the day's new information, knowing what to keep and what to throw away so you can have a productive afternoon of work.

3 p.m.–7 p.m. (Water)

Water's "high tide" is late afternoon and early evening. First the **bladder** receives and stores what you will later need. In the Chinese system, as we have seen, the bladder acts as a reservoir. It keeps reserves of fluid throughout your body, for your joints, your digestive system, your sexual excretions and tears. Many people experience a dip of energy in late afternoon because their reserves are low. If you are living by the natural clock and drinking enough water, late afternoon will be a time when you feel buoyed up.

The **kidneys** benefit at 5 p.m., when the body and mind's reserves are consolidated and you have a heightened experience of your own existence, and a profound sense of your "essential self."

7 p.m.–11 p.m. (Fire)

The fire element is unique in that it's the only one of the five elements that has not only two organs (heart and small intestine) but also two "functions." Now, at 7 p.m., it's time for the circulation-sex/heart protector function to come to the fore, a period for relaxation, socializing and sex. And for being with other people. Interestingly, this time is the resting period of the stomach when this organ has the least energy available to it. Unfortunately most of us have our biggest meal of the day at this hour. Is it any wonder our sex lives suffer?

The second stage is ruled by the "three heater" function, or the body's heating engineer, busily traveling around every part of our being, adjusting and correcting the physical and emotional temperature. It brings you down from the heat and activity of the day to a cool, resting state ready for deep restorative sleep.

11 p.m.–3 a.m. (Wood)

Think of the **gall bladder** as the "night train" that departs at 11 p.m. and takes us back to our roots, a place of deep rest. It is said, "an hour before midnight is worth two thereafter."

From 1 a.m. to 3 a.m. is the **liver**'s peak time. It receives and detoxifies the blood. The liver presides over sleep and is the dream state where our unconscious mind explores and plans for the next day. "Let me sleep on it," we commonly say, when we need time to reflect and access the "vision" of wood and the liver.

What I found humbling about the Law of Midday/Midnight when I first learned about it was that it made me feel for once that I didn't have to be completely in charge of everything. It also made me realize that there is an enormous intelligence at play keeping me alive while I am running around living my life.

In the West we're told we have the choice and freedom to work everything out for ourselves. Sometimes that freedom promotes arrogance or an exaggerated sense of responsibility, both of which are counterproductive. Your body and organs already know how they will best function, and how to give you the full life experience. If we live in accordance with the natural laws and nature's clock it all falls into place, and it's less of a struggle. Notice that the Chinese Clock has nothing to say about having to eat salmon or jogging for 30 minutes a day. There's room for flexibility, but you have to acknowledge that by not working with this "law" you're not doing yourself any favors when the stakes are high for your health.

This is a great opportunity for you to be grateful for Natural Law and to accept gracefully your proper place in the world. This surrender is a step in the right direction when it comes to climbing up the pendulum and finding your way Home.

Love and enjoy your body. Don't take it for granted. Look after it as you would your most cherished friend, partner, child or pet. Listen to what it asks of you, and tells you, and have an awareness of the cast of heroes (your organs and functions) who work tirelessly to give you the opportunity to be alive and stay in touch with the natural flow. When your attention is on your body you are here and now. You "Know" you exist. This is the first ripple of Truth that emanates from Home: "Knowledge of Existence is Bliss."

"Only love is real."

SATYANANDA

This step represents full immersion in body; a purification and a further abstraction from the limitations of "I," and a direct experience of Love through your physical form.

When your full attention is on your body, your senses are sharpened, and you have an awareness of the organs and functions that maintain your life—this tangible experience is called Love. I am talking here not of the romantic love we normally associate with the word, but the wider and more expansive Love that produces your life and maintains our world.

To return to the Tao for a moment: life begins when form emerges from the Tao—formless space. You are the outcome of this benevolent act of grace, which is the origin of the five elements and the source of everything we experience and know in creation. The ancient Chinese saw this movement of life as the ultimate cause, and the virtuous guidance that maintains life. As Lao Tzu, the founder of philosophical Taoism, put it, "When a man has perfect virtue, fire cannot burn him, water cannot drown him, cold and heat cannot afflict him, birds and beasts cannot injure him. I do not say that he makes light of these things. I mean that he distinguishes between safety and danger, contents himself with fortune or misfortune, and is cautious in his comings and goings. Therefore nothing can harm him."

The Tao is Love. It is formless and indestructible and becomes conscious of itself as it manifests as the five elements (our physical form), each one producing the next in an endless creative cycle. The wood demonstrates *benevolence* through its generous act of birth and rebirth, the fire maintains *propriety* and order through its maturing nature and the earth demonstrates *integrity* by giving form and stability. Metal's *righteousness* maintains the quality of the connection to the Source, and water provides *wisdom* through its capacity to absorb Love and stimulate the next cycle through the benevolence of wood.

The challenge at this stage on our journey is to surrender. We are—all of us—a blend of form and formlessness, and our challenge is to surrender and experience the two as One. There is no individuality or differentiation at this level—we are "One."

"Giving up" your mind and "I" is hard—in fact, impossible. But as I said at the beginning of this book, "choice" is all about where you put your attention, and so in real terms you're not giving up anything. At Step 7 you shift your attention fully to your body through your senses, to make a deep connection with the vibration of Love. By putting all your attention on your body and its capacity to see, hear, smell, feel and taste—you will find the "bridge" that will help you to not only cross over from the World of Body to the World of Home, but to experience the source and purity of Love radiating from above.

Having dropped the "sandbags" of your thoughts behind you, the relative lightness of your physical "being" lifts you like a hot-air balloon. The body is Love, just as everything in manifestation is a mirror of the Love found at the height of the pendulum and Home.

Our original and only problem is that we doubt and question the miracle and the purity of Love at "Home." With every "thought" (and all thoughts begin with "I") we create our world, our world of conditional love and peace, and in this self-created realm, rooted in duality, we forget about the Light and get lost in the shadows.

"The effects of Love are maximal. While the problems of the world can be extremely complicated, the miracle represents a divine intercession from a thought system beyond our own, and is absolute in its power. Love takes precedence over the illusions of the world. Miracles occur naturally as expressions of love." MARIANNE WILLIAMSON

Love's light banishes the shadows and, as we offer up our willful mind to the light of Home, Love's maximal power supersedes all problems of the illusory world.

Step 7 is Love and Home on earth—your physicality—your world. It is your key to the door of Home. Turn off your phone, disconnect the Internet, pull the curtains and sit quietly so that you can tune into your senses and experience that which exists within.

Are you sitting comfortably? Let's start with two very simple questions.

1. Are you aware of your own existence? Do you exist?
2. Can you feel (with your senses) that you have a physical form? Does your body exist?

If you have answered "yes" to both these questions, you are experiencing Love and you are ready to pass over to the World of Home.

If you answered "no" then you are thinking—read on, and at the end of this step, ask your Self, and *not* your mind, these two questions once again.

For the ancient Chinese, it was simple: "Love" was life itself—the gift of this planet, the rising of the sun, even one's own existence—everything is Love. Love was seen as the active part of life that powered evolution and was benevolent in every way. The creation in spring and the destruction in autumn—the essential balance of these two seasons that turned each year and maintained life—for them was Love and a Loving act. When we observe nature, we see the creative cycle of the elements and how each element emerges from the unconditional Love-thrust of the previous element—the original mother/child relationship. By observing how nature creates a cycle that is so absolutely Loving, giving and effortlessly flowing, we understand that what occurs within us occurs not because of us, but in spite of us.

Love is the power of creation and is permanently present and available to us at all times. If we are unloving, or feel unloved, then either we have lost our connection with Home, or we have taken the misguided step of thinking we could do it alone.

The ancient Chinese had a sophisticated allegorical understanding of how Love manifests in humans. The "utmost source"—an acupuncture point on the heart meridian (channel)—receives the source of Love, the "mandate of heaven," and through our own little love factory inside, the circulation/sex function, it generates unconditional Love for our Self and everyone we meet. What this ancient wisdom teaches us is that "We" are Love.

When you cross Step 7 you begin to awaken to your Self. You'll be as free as a butterfly that emerges from a chrysalis, leaving the husk of mind and body behind.

At Step 7, the intensity of the call to Home is "heard" loud and clear in every cell of our physical Being. Our attention shifts to whence it came. The more unburdened we are, the clearer the signal we receive. The more quiet and still we are, the more we will hear and Know.

THE WORLD OF HOME

Being

"No matter where you go, there you are."
YOGI BERRA

The World of Home has three steps and then you've made it—you're at the top and "Home." The swing of the pendulum at this stage of the journey is further reduced and will eventually become negligible; Peace and stillness are their defining characteristics.

This final part of the journey home is designed to transition you and deliver you safely back to your Self and Home. But before we move, I'd like you to pause and consolidate by reflecting on how far you've come.

Many people rarely question themselves in any way at all. Life is so full and rushed, it can be a challenge just to get through it. "I have no time," they say, "to start examining myself." They assume that the way they are and their perception of the world are "normal" and unlikely to change. The idea that life could be any different from the way it currently is does not seem possible. What I have asked you to do in this book is radical. I have asked you to step back and examine yourself with openness, honesty and compassion. In the first step in the World of Mind you challenged your identity and the notion of "I." In the following four steps you looked at the nature of your mind as an instrument that can both serve you *and* control you and saw that this awareness alone could set you free. In the World of Body, with the help of five-element law, you broke down the character/personality traits that you thought were the full and fixed story of you, and saw that this limited view was only a small part of the much bigger picture of you. You came to understand that Natural Law is immutable and that this divine edict that governs your physical being is there to maintain your existence as you enjoy the greatest gift of all—the gift of life through Love.

Now you have the opportunity to take the final steps to return to home base and know what it is to be truly free. Free of your thoughts, free of your body and to know the bliss of being at One with your Self.

We're naturally drawn to Home because in truth we never left. Home is where we live inside ourselves, permanently. Having climbed up the pendulum shaft, we can look down and see our other, former life below for what it is: something impermanent and constantly moving and in flux.

"Reality" is a relative concept. When we go about our daily lives, dealing with the stuff of life, having a multitude of thoughts and feelings—this is what we call reality. We're all greatly invested in what we collectively agree is real. We love to talk about our "real life." "I must get back to real life," we say, when we've taken a few days' break. Or "get real," we cry, when someone steps out of line and suggests a different way.

And then we go to bed and dream. In the dream world we enter a new reality and for as long as we are dreaming—*this* is real. "I didn't realize I was rich and famous," we marvel as we enter our stately home. Then we wake up and say, "Oh, it was just a dream"—and go straight back to work where the other "reality" kicks back in. We all agree on what is real and what is a dream, because our logical minds are conditioned to tell us so.

These final steps will help you rediscover the Home inside your Self where your problematic everyday life will be seen for what it is—relatively speaking—a dream!

We exist on many levels and all are "real" within their own context. It is pointless to try intellectually or philosophically to dismiss one over the other as it all depends on where your attention lies when you choose to label something. Within the world of duality, you and your problems *are* "real," but when seen from Home they're part of a dreamworld.

Carl Jung "really" got this when he uttered, "*Who looks outside, dreams. Who looks inside, awakens.*"

"It's like a finger pointing away to the moon.
Don't concentrate on the finger or you will
miss all that heavenly glory."
BRUCE LEE

Step 8 is your first step into the World of Home and the turning point of the journey. For some readers this gear change may be difficult. But stay with me and let's take it slowly—I'm here to guide you as you take a leap of faith. This is the moment when you retreat from your mind and turn to face the loving light of Home and begin to awaken to your Self.

Leaving behind the endless cycle of opposites

Up until this point everything we have looked at exists by the grace of duality—i.e. everything that exists in thought and name has an opposite. In ancient Chinese philosophy, as we saw in Step 6, this occurrence is known as Yin-Yang, and this "reality" is evidenced in everything we know: hot–cold, war–peace, boy–girl, love–hate.

All form, including the body *and* the mind, is an outcome of the law of opposites in action and can only exist within this law. As one thought arises it gives birth to the opposite, offering choice, and one path is chosen—free will! For example, we may think, "I'll go to bed now," and simultaneously another thought arises—"Well, maybe not." And then we make our choice. This is also known as the law of cause and effect, or karma, where every choice we take presents an outcome, which in itself becomes the new cause in an ongoing chain of events that shapes the overall path of our total life experience. Most of these subtle thoughts and choices go unnoticed by the conscious mind—but they go on throughout the waking day and the dreaming state. This law of opposites also gives rise to "time," and is the mechanism that creates and maintains the physical universe.

*Every thought you have has "form" and is bound by the law of cause and effect. Every thought has an outcome—**spoken or not**.*

If you accept Step 8's offer and trade your thoughts for "Love," you need to become aware of the following: that when your mind (bound by the law of opposites) encounters the purity of Love (the Source of all things), in an attempt to "understand" and absorb this state of grace, it will try and separate Love and create the lower and divided states of love and hate. At the threshold of Step 8, you have a choice: you can choose to stay bound in the world of duality and opposites, and exist as part of free will; or you can choose to retreat from your mind and pass this step—where Love is all there is.

This is why Step 8 is so hard to cross. We believe in our mind and body as the only reality and we've been conditioned to believe in the power of choice. Do you love or hate? Pride can attach to either side and often the exact same action arises from both—i.e. it is both loving and hateful. This has been our problem since we attached to thoughts and bought into the illusion of "I think, therefore I am." We cannot pass Step 8 as long as we only believe in our divided world—the confused and conflicted world of love and hate—the World of Mind. The thing we love one day, we hate the next. We are caught in the *endless cycle of opposites*.

It is in the nature of the mind to change. "Home," however, does not change, and nor does the purity of Love which is undivided and undividable.

When we find our way and live our life from Home, our point of perception is changed. The former knee-jerk reflex to mentally judge and separate things feels empty and pointless and the need to compare, fight and reinforce a sense of self through the rejection of others feels futile and unkind. When we look out from Home and we see our fellow human beings as "One," we transcend the restrictive parameters of a life lived exclusively from the duality of the mind.

This leap of faith is hard when you're addicted to your thoughts and so you may need some kind of ceremony or ritual to help you take this step.

Many religions have rituals and stories, which serve to "point" the way Home. One parable you may be familiar with is when Jesus told his disciples, "*It is easier for a camel to go through the eye of a needle than for a rich man to enter the kingdom of God.*" My understanding of this famous quote in the context of taking this leap of faith and finding your way Home is this: as long as you believe your thoughts to be the only reality, you carry them on your back like precious and valued possessions. But acquired and stored knowledge is a burden. In the process of returning Home and finding permanent Peace, Step 8 ensures you are sufficiently unburdened—having thrown off the false construct of who you "think" you are—to pass through the "eye of the needle," as an act of faith. Purification in this context is to be free of thoughts, ideas and labels—to Know your Self as Love.

This does not mean you disappear into a puff of smoke and that everything you ever knew vanishes. It doesn't mean you become saintly and only have good thoughts—quite the opposite.

Your bad habits, your phobias and fears from childhood, your dislikes, your passions, your gifts—everything about you remains as behavior or as memory but it is now seen from the non-judgment of Home. You see the wonder and the enormity of "You," and from this elevated vantage point you view the uniqueness of your life—with equanimity and compassion. You are free.

CASE STUDY—ROBERT

Robert came to me suffering from what he described as an "inexcusable depression." To all intents and purposes, he said, he had a perfect life. Or certainly an incredibly privileged one. But he felt lost: "I knew I was living a life that most people would dream of, but I couldn't feel it. I had a wonderful partner, a beautiful house and an exciting job. I also had a low-level depression that had been with me from as early as I could remember. I had sought this amazing life in the belief that peace and happiness would then finally find me, and drive away the ever-nagging lows. They didn't—in fact, I felt worse as I now had a huge dose of guilt thrown in. Guilt based on the fact that I knew I was one of the luckiest beings on this planet, yet I could not feel it. I was unhappier than ever."

My work with him centered on trying to get him to face his nameless fears, to take a leap of faith, and trust himself. It was hard for him, a man who had "created" what he had deemed in his wisdom to be his own little realm of perfection; and for a while he got very low. But then, quite suddenly, something began to shift in him.

"From a breakdown of sorts I started to let go and try literally to follow my heart and stop judging everything; just do those things that felt right. With this as my guide, I then had a series of experiences which were life-changing. These events awakened me to the realization that true happiness starts within and this is an old and ancient truth . . . We are all connected and interconnected.

"I realized that my journey and my experiences were as old as the hills, and not necessarily simply a first world problem. What a relief! The ever-present depression slipped away and I woke up . . . Things were no longer conditional, half empty or half full, and I could feel genuine happiness and Love for the first time."

Faith, meditation and prayer

Whether we accept it or not, we all have faith. Some have faith in the power of their vitamin pills, some in their intellect, the skill of their doctor or the magic of the acupuncture needles—and some in God. Faith is part of being human and it is not prescriptive but its essence is rooted deep within us. When it feels like something's wrong in our life (in spite of having ticked all the boxes), and we end up feeling alone in the world and that we have to work it all out for ourselves, we become separated from the faith within us. "If we can just maintain control we will be okay," we think.

> To pass Step 8 and reach the Peace of Home, you need to let go of the idea that you are somehow in control of achieving happiness through your mind. You need to give up the belief that you need knowledge to exist——to have a willingness, in short, to no longer believe in your beliefs.
>
> Faith is different to belief. Belief comes from the mind and is a calculation that can fall on one side of the fence or the other. It can divide opinion and can change. Faith emerges from our Self and is a total surrender to what "Is" and the cessation of any judgment. Belief is divisive. Faith is unifying.

Meditation, prayer or any form of "surrender" ritual act as "spiritual keys," or pointers to a more humble state—ways to enter the door of Home. It would be a terrible shame were you to almost complete this journey, having read, digested and absorbed every nugget of "information" in this book, only to find as you arrive at the door that you've forgotten to collect the key.

Julianne, a patient, spent many years believing she was lost, and shares her experience here: "I have always known where I wanted to live: I want to live in the home which is mine to inhabit. To walk in and take refuge, to drink deeply from what I constructed to care for myself. I have always known what my four walls would be: to make a positive contribution, to love deeply, to have a spiritual practice and to heal and repair my little corner of the world. But I was dying under the weight of my story, my tight grip on every injury that I nursed and let define me. The suffering was so deep that I did what we all do; I used things around me to numb my pain. I began to separate from my Self and I lost the keys to my house. I would see my home as wrapped in mist, me stumbling around looking for the door. To be homeless is to be consigned to a half-life. It is unbearable for any sentient being."

There's a lot of discomfort around the idea of rituals, meditation and prayer in nonreligious circles. It's often seen as a bit weird and for desperate people only, or for people controlled by religious doctrine or worse still those "slackers" who take no responsibility for themselves and expect something or someone else to look after them.

But let's look at it another way. It's tough for people to admit they need help, and even harder to actually ask for it, because we've been educated to believe we have to be independent, strong and self-reliant and the thought of getting down on your knees, two palms pressed together, is not in tune with the "can do" vibe that most of us head to bed with before privately stressing and struggling all night long, only to embark on another day of hunting and searching.

The truth is we search. That's what we do. And whether it's a promotion, a new home, a meaningful book, or a better way of life, the search goes on and it is rare that we meet anyone who can hand on heart say that they are "found" and the search is over. Most of us accept this life of confusion as the norm and try to keep our mind busy as it chaotically looks for answers. We're fixated on the "pointing finger" that's showing us where to look.

Well, here at Step 8, we can give up the hunt and accept that we're done—we're already here, and we're okay.

Taking this leap of faith is scary. We'd rather run back to what we know (the searching)—after all, for many of us it's not that bad—and yet it's not good enough—and so the search goes on . . .

Meditation and prayer (in the spiritual sense) are an acknowledgment that there is something greater than us; greater than what we can know through our thinking mind. I have friends who say, "Yes, I agree with you. I love to stop thinking and just be in nature—that's my religion," and they go and visit it occasionally in a park or on holiday, but this is still an experience outside of themselves.

We all need a method or ritual to help us shift our attention from the outside in—away from our mind to our Self. The moment our attention resides at Home the search is over and the mind starved of attention naturally quiets and assumes its role of serving the Self.

Yes, I can hear you thinking, this is all very interesting—but how do I actually do it? The answer is simple:

Before enlightenment, chop wood, carry water. After enlightenment, chop wood, carry water.   ZEN PARABLE

This parable, so beautiful in its simplicity, tells us that enlightenment has nothing to do with changing anything. Enlightenment is beyond the mundane tasks of life but is found within them. You don't need to sit on a mountain and chant, or give away all your possessions to find your Self—you simply need to Be your Self —but don't forget to "carry water, chop wood."

And if your thoughts keep running and you get confused, pause, and ask yourself this simple question with all your heart: "Who am I?" The realization that you cannot answer the mind's first question is enough to return you directly to Home.

I first experienced the joy of what I can only describe as an epiphany as a boy, when I was sent on a two-week residential course for young singers. Something happened to me on that course that I still find hard to explain. But it was certainly prompted by what I was reading.

I'd been given the box set of Narnia books for my birthday and consumed them while I was away. I knew nothing about the deeper spiritual meaning of Lewis's iconic books but I do remember, quite out of the blue while reading the section where Aslan the Lion offers to sacrifice himself, becoming acutely aware of my physical presence, coupled with a deep sense of peace.

This feeling lasted for the whole of the following week. And my parents, surprised, and then somewhat discomforted by my new, and strangely benign, presence, challenged me with religious-conversion jokes until I finally broke, and decided to give up peace—and take up smoking.

It was some years before I reconnected with my spiritual Self. I moved to California in my early 20s and after a relatively hedonistic few years, I realized I needed to do something about my health. California in the 1980s was a hotbed of new age thinking, alternative ideas, therapies and discussion groups, giving me plenty of opportunities to investigate my burgeoning need to find a new way of living. And at this time I started a very simple meditation practice which I learned from a small scrappy paperback book I'd found in a secondhand bookstore. It taught me to sit quietly and shift my attention to my breath and the sensation of my bare feet on the floor. Just that.

As part of my ongoing spiritual education, I have spent many years reading and re-reading *The Sermon on the Mount* by Emmet Fox. In this book, Dr. Fox, a spiritual leader and teacher during the Great Depression in New York City, explains in depth the message that Jesus taught on the mount, from a metaphysical point of view rather than from a religious perspective. He also explains that the "prayer" was given by Jesus in response to being asked how to pray. The prayer he gave is a "spiritual key" and a gift to humanity—and very possibly one way Home.

I am not a "Christian," nor do I align myself with any organized religion. In fact my only formal study in any vaguely religious area was a three-year training in the Kabbalah, an esoteric form of Judaism. But I am fascinated and intrigued by any philosophy that focuses on the nature of "Being" or "Knowing."

Jesus the man, the Rabbi, was clearly brilliant and a wonderful communicator of Truth and in spite of the Chinese whispers that have gone on over the centuries, his enduring message of forgiveness and that "the Kingdom of God is within" is unimpeachable: that by coming Home to your Self you will find the Peace and Love you have been searching for your entire life.

There is no one way to meditate or pray. I have evolved

all sorts of different methods or "keys" over the years. I would not say practice makes perfect, but it does certainly make one better at it, and I now find it relatively easy to be able to shift my attention away from my thoughts to a deep sense of peace, almost wherever I am. During some sittings, a profound shift occurs. I shift from my mind, to my body, and then to what I can only describe as a void. In this sanctum "thoughts" cannot enter, and, even though I am aware of them peripherally, they cannot intrude on this space. The image I have is that of a fishbowl over my head and the fish (my thoughts) are tapping on the glass but can't get back in.

By contemplating the metaphysical message of the Lord's prayer, I have developed a mantra which when recited helps me shift my awareness from my mind and body to the stillness and sanctity of Home.

We are spiritual beings
We are Truth and beyond the mundane
Our Self is our Home
Home is the source of our humanity and sustenance
Forgiveness and compassion are the way Home.

I share this experience not because I want you to follow my particular path, but rather to encourage you to find your own ritual or rituals and a way Home that resonates with you. Sometimes we forget key moments in life that serve as pointers to Truth; we dismiss them as odd coincidences or we hide them for fear that people will judge us for being "daft," but a gentle nudge might stir a memory in you that carries the freshness of that time and awaken a part of you denied until now.

If not—don't worry. The epiphany is here and now and all you have to do is wake up to the reality of the permanent Peace that is "You."

Maybe, to start with, you could simply sit and spend time with your Self. Think about whatever you like—it's not possible to stop your thoughts, but be aware of shifting your attention to the One who witnesses your thinking.

A spiritual teacher whose groups I attend was once asked this simple question. "Is it necessary to meditate to follow a spiritual path?" The teacher paused for a while and then answered. "If you still think you're somebody—then yes."

Remember those mind games?

Meditation or prayer is a vehicle to shift our attention from the thinking mind to the Being Self. But one of the great difficulties that people encounter when embarking on a meditation practice is to know the difference between a peaceful *mind* and the peace of Being; or as we have come to learn—the relative peace at the base of the pendulum and Absolute Peace found at the top.

When we're successful at meditation, we experience "Bliss"—even if it is only momentary. But we need to be "mindful" of the difference between unconditional peace and conditional peace. The mind (as always) records this seemingly fleeting experience and stores it as memory and through the body's capacity to produce endorphins around any experience, a "faux" experience can be re-produced each time the ritual of meditation is employed. The mind takes the *complete* experience of Being, and re-cords it as a *separate* experience to revisit at will. So how can we know the difference? How can we tell if our mind has thrown down a snake as we seek the ladder? How do we know if we are at Home or simply calming our mind?

The purity of Home is permanent and complete and the only reason it seems fleeting is that it is we (our minds) who come and go.

The sense that Bliss is a temporary state is a trick of the mind that will draw us back down to thought, and produce a "good" feeling—an endorphin high.

Remember that the mind's offering is always temporary and conditional whereas the Peace and Bliss of Home are permanent and unconditional.

Step 8 is the hand of Grace. It is an invitation to transcend your current point of perception—and add a whole other dimension to your own experience of existence. Nothing has to change on the outside but your attention shifts to the inside as you pass through the "eye of the needle" to enter the World of Home and discover your Self. The key insight here is to surrender. Let go of every thought, belief, opinion—and all knowledge— and you'll still be here. Leave your expectations, your resentments, your attitudes behind and bask in the freedom that Step 8 provides.

*"There are two things that are infinite, the
universe and man's stupidity . . .
And I am not sure about the universe."*
ALBERT EINSTEIN

*"Out beyond ideas of wrongdoing and rightdoing,
there is a field.
I will meet you there.
When the soul lies down in that grass,
the world is too full to talk about
language, ideas, even the phrase 'each other'
doesn't make any sense."*
RUMI

Up until this point you've probably spent the best part of your life worrying about doing the right or the wrong thing. With all the best intentions, just when you thought you were getting it right someone changed the rules and a "right" became a "wrong" and a "wrong" became a "right" and "you do the hokey pokey and you turn about," yes! That is what it's all about—the game of endlessly trying to get it right while tirelessly avoiding getting it wrong! It's so exhausting and confusing—the world of thoughts and morals.

Here at Step 9 we have transcended the world of opposites, the building blocks of thought and form. Here, judgments rise—*but* fall. "Right and wrong" along with "love and hate" are at the door and cannot come in. They're there for you to collect on your way out, but in the peace and sanctity of Home there's no room for poor little "right" and "wrong"—they'll just have to sit and wait.

Once we enter the space of Home, we are in a place where nothing matters, not in the sense of having become immoral beings, but because we are *prior* to and *beyond* morality. This idea can be difficult for many of us to accept at first glance, but there is nothing nihilistic about it: I say nothing matters in the sense that everything is okay. From this new perspective we forgive and we are forgiven. We know in our hearts that permanent Peace and the key to the door of Home are only found by retreating from our mind and its dogged habit of questioning and judging Truth.

This step is familiar but feels new. We remember how it is to be free of our mind, but our habit is to *think* and so we're strangers to peace and *being* "at Home." We now need to be vigilant so that we do not slip again.

The nonsense our mind conjures up is frightening when you realize that the stability of our world is dependent on this brilliant but contrary and conflicted tool. So if at this point of the book you're still not clear what's real, what's right and what's wrong—here's the answer.

> *Nothing you can know from your mind will ever be the whole Truth—and come the day that we all wake up to our Self and Home, there'll be no need for right or wrong.*

"What?" you protest. "But we need a moral code. Surely if there was no such thing as right or wrong we'd all be killing and stealing from each other." Actually, ever since Moses descended the mountain and legitimized our minds' hunger for right and wrong—we've been lost. For all the commandments that shape our lives, the rules and laws, the guidelines, punishments, public judgments and our moral code—we're *still* in chaos and possibly more confused than ever before.

Mahatma Gandhi said, "If you change your self you will change your world. If you change how you think then you will change how you feel and what actions you take. And so the world around you will change."

When we return Home—this is that "change." Change is a natural outcome when we shift our point of perception to the Home space. When we see the world from Love—the world mirrors Love. That's how we "change" the world.

When you live from Home you live from Love. You no longer worry or "mind" (literally) what happens because all outcomes that emerge from this place have been bleached of all perceived failings and character faults and related actions. The Bliss of being at Home and enjoying your life from here is a far more profound and enthralling experience than living exclusively through your mind and the lower states of right and wrong. Rather than splitting and separating the events (past and present) of your life, ruthlessly shredding an unfolding world—you sit in Peace and observe events as they play out with innocent curiosity and awe.

Let's go back to one of our questions on morality as seen from Home. Is murder okay? Can I steal something from you?

Firstly, when at Home these questions don't arise, and secondly, even if they did arise they don't compute. Why would you want to murder someone when you live from Love? Why would you want to steal from someone when that person is You, and what they have is Yours? Murder and theft (to take just two) are actions that arise from a belief that we are separate from each other, which itself arises from the insanity of the mind. Why do we generally not kill people? Is it because someone told us it is wrong? Of course it's not. We are not inclined to kill each other because our Loving human hearts beat louder and more brightly than the mechanical motor of the human mind and so for the most part we Love, value and respect each other. When we do harm—our attention has shifted to the mind and its "justifiable" actions are based on illusion, confusion, and labels, certainly not Love.

What we call morality is not morality at all. The mind hijacked Love and created the "moral code," claiming it as its own. True "morality" is that human beings Know somewhere deep inside that they are One and that they exist by the grace of Love. Love does not exist in an either/or state. Love is love and is uncompromisable.

Living in a world bound by right and wrong and cause and effect is a challenge, but only if we believe that's all there is. When we engage with life from Home, these polar dynamics that create and shape our thoughts, our feelings and our life become fascinating and profoundly rewarding. When we are firmly rooted in Love, they become the joyful dance of life.

This mechanism or movement that right and wrong create is what originally took us away from Home, and it is this same mechanism that will direct us back there. If we could only hold back from putting our attention on what we think *should* be unfolding and stop the habit of thinking we are powerful beings influencing nature unfold—we'd all have a much easier ride.

Nothing has gone wrong (or right), everything is on track, but our mind thinks it knows better and that is why we suffer. We are continuously looking for ways to improve or work out what next to do. There's nothing to do, since it's happening whether we get out of bed or not. The reading and the writing of this book are not individually inspired acts—these activities, like everything else, are just another aspect of consciousness becoming conscious of its Self.

For some people, finding their way back to the peace of Home takes a whole lifetime; and for some, this awakening to the Truth of who they are passes them by as their body fades away.

Step 10 is the moment we "die" as we live. We are free. Free from who we think we are and the burden of identity as we retain our physical form.

MY GREAT FRIEND ANNE was free and wasn't afraid of physical death—in fact she really couldn't believe it was happening to her. "It's so weird. They say I'm dying, but I feel okay," she told me, her mouth smiling, her eyes sad. She'd been diagnosed with lung cancer only a few weeks before and apart from some shortness of breath—as she said, she felt fine.

Anne was from a working-class farming community in Ireland, one of many children, the daughter of an alcoholic and at times abusive father ("That was normal in them days," she'd say) and she had left home when she was 14 years old.

She came to London and worked as a chambermaid and very quickly found her feet. She'd tell me about the signs hanging on boardinghouse doors that trumped her arrival as she looked for somewhere to live. "No Dogs. No Blacks. No Irish." She was proud of her roots but had also bought into the idea that she would never be quite good enough. And yet in spite of this she was determined to find her way and create a life for herself that matched how she felt inside.

There was a bright and magnificent light inside Anne and the life she created matched the beauty of her core. She married, had five children, made the most elegant home, and most strikingly became the magical, mythical aunt we'd all love to have but rarely ever find. If anyone had a problem, "Go see Anne," we'd say. "She'll sort you out."

Anne loved to love, and although in many ways she was naive and charmingly unaware, she was also fiercely on the money when it came to authenticity and truth. She couldn't stand anything disingenuous—she'd sniff it out in seconds. "Jesus—you really are a very selfish man—aren't you?" she once said to me with a smile.

The message cut deep but left no scar—her skill of targeting the "bullshit," calling you on your stuff, and then extracting it with love was like the work of a master surgeon.

Anne loved the pendulum. We discovered it together right after we met on the first day at our psychotherapy training course. Anne understood its power long before me and whenever we reminisced, she'd relate it to the pendulum: "Oh we had such fun last night and the drink was good, but I was high, high, high—so I'm doing all I can to come back to the calm." She'd had a problem with alcohol at various points in her life but the pendulum had helped her understand the volatility of her thoughts and emotions and she knew that the very things she craved the most, laughter and joy, were also the source of de-structive behavior—first in the high and then in an ex-tended exile in the low.

Anne was either sad or happy—I rarely saw her any other way, but poignantly she was at Peace and okay in herself no matter what she felt on the surface. She lived from Home. She'd eventually found her way to the calm, up there at the top of the pendulum—to such an extent that even when death stared her in the face, her impend-ing demise did little more than gently swing her from sweet sadness to beguiling joy. "I'm going to float out the window—that way," she repeated many times to me in the last weeks of her life, and her bruised and with-ered arm would lift as she'd point out of the window in the direction of her flight, her long red nails reaching to the sky.

"I've been so lonely," she'd tell me. "So lonely. But me? I'm good."

I was saddened to hear Anne repeat this many times

but I couldn't escape what she had taught me over the two decades of knowing her personally and professionally. She was okay *in spite of* being lonely—this was her thing.

Culturally, we place a lot of importance on the value of certain emotions in our life. We have created a hierarchy of good and bad emotions with a clear division between them; and God help us if we get stuck on the wrong side of the fence; but Anne taught me that it actually doesn't matter what you're feeling—they're just ephemeral emotions, here one day, gone the next.

Whatever feeling or experience you shared with Anne she'd celebrate. "I feel so depressed," you'd confess. "Brilliant," she'd say, and take your hand in hers. "I am just very angry," and again, "Brilliant," she'd say. "Wonderful! Just go for it—scream the house down," and she'd laugh. Even fear, shame, guilt and jealousy were okay in the house of Anne. Everything was welcome in the presence of her unconditional Love. She helped us all understand that there is room for everything—every thought and feeling has a right to exist.

Anne was thoroughly human. This was her gift. When you were in the presence of Anne—you enjoyed your Self. You loved to be you—you with all your odd and quirky bits and bobs out in the open to be examined and played with, like children with their toys.

KEY INSIGHT

There is a place inside your Self where wrong
and right do not exist.
Let's all meet there.
Where We lie down together with nothing to say.
The intense Bliss of Home gives no room for debate.
All thoughts and feelings, even the notion
of "us" cannot take form.

"What you seek is seeking you."
RUMI

The incredible lightness of Being

Finding your way Home is really just a good old-fashioned love story. It's about falling head over heels in love with your Self.

You know when you're madly in love with someone, in the flush of the honeymoon phase—you'll do anything to be with that person. You're happy to empty the trash together, to be stuck in traffic together, you'll even change your whole life to be together. Everything is second to the experience of Being with the one you Love.

When you find the way Home, there's nothing more you want to do than to be with the one you Love. In this context Home is where you want to be; it's who "You" really are. This is one love affair where the honeymoon never ends.

Step 10 is the point of changed perception. Looking out from Home, you see the totality of who You are—but now everything about you that was previously separated and judged is seen only from Love. Your heart is empty and you are free. You are light and unburdened.

Falling madly in Love with your Self is Home. Knowing the whole Truth of your existence—in essence, form and thought—is utter bliss. Here we enjoy the Truth that We are One and that our uniqueness as an individual, rather than being something "separate," is just one small fraction of the wholeness of Home.

Take another look from here. View your world with curiosity and the possibility of experiencing everything from innocence and awe. Here you see the magic of your creation (your life) by grasping the possibility of starting all over again—the chance to experience life anew through the purity of your senses and the humility of your mind. Releasing your mind from the responsibility of having to judge and label sets it free. Let your body and mind gratefully bend in service to your Self.

Claire, a patient of many years, knows how it is to live from Home: "Before, I might have woken up feeling happy, or depressed or angry, but I would barely have had the self-awareness to acknowledge my moods. I was a slave to these ups and downs without even realizing it. The next stage was becoming conscious of these states, but at this point I still identified such emotions as being part of my essential self, thereby investing them with enormous power. Now, I am able to observe these changes from a distance: happy or depressed or angry, none of these are 'me.' Just like the sea may be calm or choppy or rise up in raging waves, it is always water; so am I always me, always there and always fine. I am a work in progress and it is not always easy to access this perspective of distance, but when I inhabit this place, the feeling of Peace and lightness and freedom is wonderful."

Claire is realizing the Truth of who she is, but this "success" is not a mental calculation, it is an inner Knowing—once Known never lost.

The Return

The rather odd and wonderful thing about the journey Home is that in reality "You" don't go anywhere. It's a bit like a plane journey. You get off the plane and you're in a completely different place and yet you haven't actually "gone" anywhere . . . You've just been sitting in your seat, doing nothing.

Once we're at Home we realize that who we really are and the Truth of Being are permanent, and do not move or change. We sit safely and peacefully at Home—we are in the stillness at the top of the pendulum, away from the mental drama and emotional swings of the "bob" below—and just like on the journey on a plane or on a train, we see the clouds, the fields, traffic jams and cattle pass us by . . . but We are the same.

"The Return" is the great news that You can now go back to life knowing that it's not yours to own or control or change. This awakening is the key to freedom, and the pendulum will keep you on track. My patient Peter was delighted to realize this was the outcome of coming Home, having feared he'd have to abandon the life he loved if he wanted to find permanent peace.

"I've learned that you can have it all. The secret: care immensely—and don't care at all. I'm a highly committed senior advertising exec. I use my job and career as a way to define who I am; it is part of my identity and how I project myself to other people. I recently took a new job at one of the world's top agencies and I absolutely love it. It's high-pressure, high-profile and high-stakes. However, if the whole thing finished next week and I was sacked I wouldn't honestly care. If I never worked again it would give me the time to enjoy the peace I have with myself. What's most valuable? I'm not sure, but they both feel really 'good.'"

The idea of "returning" is an abstract one and we use this word to support the idea of going on a journey somewhere (Home) and then re-emerging, having rested, and ready to take on the world from a more balanced and healthier perspective.

"The Return" is our commitment to be open to everything and everyone, to not limit ourselves; to not imprison ourselves again.

As I have said several times before in this book—true freedom is the freedom to *not* be free—and now we are Home it will be easier to take this on as Truth.

"Take me, handcuff me and put me in your cell, I just don't care. Tell me I'm bad and that you disapprove of who you think I am. Go on—put any label on me—I don't mind at all." FREEDOM

Jesus famously said, "Father, forgive them for they know not what they do," when he was judged and convicted and put on the cross. Jesus didn't mind—he didn't care for himself because he was at Home and beyond the primitive world of thought and judgment. Out of compassion for those bound tightly by the old law of cause and effect, he could only see his perpetrators as lost and conflicted souls who needed to make him "wrong" to make themselves feel "right." When Jesus had "good" and forgiving thoughts about the very people who mocked, jeered and gambled for his clothes—his goodness was not in the face of badness, it came from a place where badness has neither permanence nor truth.

When we're resident at Home we don't "mind," and we don't care what anyone says or does to us—because we are free. This doesn't mean that we don't suffer and experience the naturally arising thoughts and emotions that one would expect from a terrible situation in our life, and it doesn't mean we don't take action or do nothing. It's rather that we are able to observe these thoughts, emotions, from a safe place, a beyond . . .

I would like to cite here the words of Eva Kor, a Holocaust survivor and a teacher for us all in finding the way Home. Eva suffered at the hands of Dr. Mengele and the Nazis while incarcerated in Auschwitz and yet found it possible, and preferable, to forgive.

"My recipe for everyone who has survived trauma is to forgive. I always emphasize that you should do it not because the perpetrator deserves forgiveness, but because the victim deserves it. The only way you can heal yourself is to forgive those who have harmed you. I call forgiveness the best revenge. Because from the time you forgive, the perpetrator no longer has the power to control you. Or we could call it the greatest gift one can give oneself: the gift of healing, freedom, and self-empowerment."

This quote is a beautiful example of someone who abides at Home but also lives in a world of suffering, reasoning and thought. When we find our way Home and forgive ourselves (our mind) for believing we're not okay—that our true Existence is somehow conditional— we have given ourselves the "gift of healing, freedom, and self-empowerment."

It can take time to fully unwrap this treasured gift. For some of you, what you have read here will have thrown light on things you have long known about yourself; for others, it may have offered a completely fresh way of looking at life. Others still among you may feel a bit alienated or confused by the message. To you I would say, don't worry; but now that you have read the book, perhaps set it down for a while and come back to it when you are ready.

In one sense, as I have said, there is nothing new for you to learn. This is, after all, a process of *un*-learning. Everything you need you have—and the process of waking up to this truth is nothing more than a gentle retreat from a former, limited perception of yourself and your life.

It's hard, I know: we're continually told the opposite.

In recent years there have been many bestselling books that promote the power of positive visualization as a means to happiness. It's tantalizing. "Project the image of your heart's desire and as if by magic it will appear before you"—and yes, this is true. The power of the mind to create is a miracle. But this experience is limited to the level of the mind and is necessarily temporary—when you live from your mind you're bound by the law of opposites. To quote our compulsive swinger Graham, "What goes up—must come down."

Conditioned as we are to believe there is only one way

or another, I hope that I have at least begun the process of freeing you from your limiting beliefs. This is a message that I myself was first deeply struck by when I read Herman Hesse's story of Siddhartha as a teenager. In his version of the story, Hesse argues that the conscious experience and appreciation of every event (good *and* bad) in a person's life is the best way to attain enlightenment.

The story tells of a young man who leaves his family believing he will not find what he is looking for at home. He sets off on his travels with a friend; they renounce material life and after many adventures find the Buddha. His friend, now satisfied, chooses to stay and follow a spiritual life. Siddhartha, however, cannot stay, as he is sure that he, and indeed all individuals, must find some *personal* meaning—something that cannot be presented by a teacher.

He continues on his journey. He finds love and riches; experiences loss, dissatisfaction, wretchedness and suicidal thoughts.

And then, at last, he finds Peace, with the realization that, after all his searching and inquiring, the answer to his question was here and now all along—it is the message found in the cycle of nature that is the key to enlightenment: nature follows its own ordered pattern and is always complete, and the separate parts of it that we see through our minds at any given time are just illusory fragments of the Oneness of Being.

It is the completeness of Siddhartha's experiences, a completeness which can only be understood when at Home in your Self, in a state of consciousness not bound by the confines of time, that ultimately sets him free, and will set you free, too. The key message of the book is that enlightenment is happening *now* and that you are complete *now*.

When we observe everything from the pivot of the pendulum we're with Siddhartha—we are at Home and we are complete. And life goes on below in its separate parts. It's a message at once beautifully simple and exhilaratingly profound.

Can you imagine if everyone knew about this—what then?

GERAD KITE

KEY INSIGHT

Be still and Know your Self.

CONCLUSION

"All conclusions come too early."
SATYANANDA

ACKNOWLEDGMENTS

I am deeply grateful to five amazing women. Clare Conville who encouraged me to write and share my work with patients. Tessa Dunlop and Charlotte Robertson who saw the value of the hidden message in my first book (*The Art of Baby Making*) and who introduced it to my publishers—Aurea Carpenter and Rebecca Nicholson— who had the vision and courage to take the message of this book and make it accessible to a wider audience.

I am eternally thankful to Johnny Childs and Wren Winfield, whose invaluable input, enthusiasm and love inform and underpin this book.

I want to express my humble and heartfelt gratitude to my teachers: Peter Fleming who introduced David Pellin's teachings and the pendulum to the UK; the late J.R. Worsley who brought Five-Element acupuncture to the West; and Satyananda (born Bernardo Lischinsky), a brilliant teacher in the tradition of Sri Ramana Maharshi, whose teachings have helped me shape the overall philosophy of this book.

Finally I want to thank my mother and my father, my extended family and everyone I have worked with in any capacity who have, without doubt, contributed to what I hope will help many people discover the greater Truth of who they really are.

ABOUT THE AUTHOR

Gerad Kite is an Acupuncture Master (AcM) with more than twenty-five years of clinical experience. He is a recognized leader in the field of infertility and an internationally respected practitioner and teacher of Worsley Five-Element Acupuncture. In 1993 he started the first-ever NHS acupuncture service at Kings College Hospital in the UK while building his private practice in central London. In 2006 he opened the Kite Clinic, where he led a large team of practitioners performing over 10,000 treatments a year, and in 2007 he founded the London Institute of Five-Element Acupuncture (LIFEA), where he personally trained his current team of practitioners. He's worked with celebrities, including John Cleese, Kate Winslet and James Corden.